THE
PSALMS
COME ALIVE

Capturing the Voice & Art of Israel's Songs

JOHN EATON

INTERVARSITY PRESS
DOWNERS GROVE, ILLINOIS 60515

©John H. Eaton 1984

Published in the United States of America by InterVarsity Press, Downers Grove, Illinois, with permission from A. R. Mowbray & Co., Ltd., England.

InterVarsity Press is the book-publishing division of Inter-Varsity Christian Fellowship, a student movement active on campus at hundreds of universities, colleges and schools of nursing. For information about local and regional activities, write IVCF, 6400 Schroeder Rd., P.O. Box 7895, Madison, WI 53707-7895.

Specified excerpts from To a Dancing God (pp. 97, 160) by Sam Keen are reprinted by permission of Harper & Row Publishers, Inc.

Cover photograph: Gary Irving

ISBN 0-87784-387-2

Printed in the United States of America

Library of Congress Cataloging in Publication Data
Eaton, J. H.
    The Psalms come alive.

    Reprint. Originally published: Oxford [Oxfordshire]:
A. R. Mowbray, c1984.
    Bibliography: p.
    Includes indexes.
    1. Bible.   O.T.   Psalms—Criticism, interpretation,
etc.   I. Title.
BS1430.2.E233   1986   223'.106   86-20115
ISBN 0-87784-387-2

17	16	15	14	13	12	11	10	9	8	7	6	5	4	3	2	1
99	98	97	96	95	94	93	92	91	90	89	88	87	86			

To my beloved
Margaret

ACKNOWLEDGEMENTS

Extracts from the Book of Common
Prayer of 1662, which is Crown
Copyright, are reproduced by
permission of Eyre & Spottiswoode,
Her Majesty's Printers, London.

An extract from W. Sorell's *Israel and
the Dance* in *The Hebrew Impact on
Western Civilisation* (ed. D. D. Runes,
1951) is reproduced by permission of
the Philosophical Library, New York.

An extract from *Vision in Worship, The
Relation of Prophecy and Liturgy in the
O.T.* by John Eaton is reproduced by
permission of SPCK, London.

LIST OF FIGURES

The illustrations have been drawn by my wife Margaret as a general guide, and she has used some reconstruction where necessary. The less commonly shown items, figures 1, 2, 11 and 13, were well presented by W. Wolf, *Das schöne Fest von Opet* (Leipzig, 1931); they are from the great processional reliefs at Luxor, now being resurveyed by the Chicago Oriental Institute.

PREFACE

It is my hope to have readers both from the student world and from the wider public. For the student, the Psalms offer the most direct way to the heart of Old Testament religion and are an indispensable complement to the histories and prophets. To the general reader, the Psalms appeal as a classic of religion and literature, as a voice for our instincts for God, and, as I try to show, as vibrant with early forms of the arts.

I have to thank Professor J. G. Davies, not only for once asking me to study Old Testament dancing for his collection of essays on *Dance and Worship*, but also for continual encouragement and for the example of his own works on worship and the arts. I am grateful also for the stimulus of having been invited to Kenyon College, Ohio, to give the Larwill Lectures, which have formed the basis of the chapter on drama. The then chairman of Kenyon's Department of Religion, Professor A. D. Baly, was also the person who introduced me to Jerusalem in 1953 – how much I owe him! Among many other scholars who have helped and inspired me over the years, I can thank here only the Revd H. St J. Hart, and Professors A. R. Johnson, G. W. Anderson and W. G. Lambert.

To Mowbrays I owe this opportunity to share my love of the Psalms, and here I am especially indebted to Canon William Purcell for his kindly advice and encouragement.

I have quoted the texts in my own translations, unless otherwise noted, as when I discuss the haunting Coverdale version of the Book of Common Prayer. 'KJ' denotes the King James or Authorized Version of 1611, and 'RSV' the Revised Standard Version of 1952. The verse numbers are those of the English Bibles.

John Eaton

1

INTRODUCTION

The adventure
I remember a morning service in Jerusalem years ago. From Psalm 87, Book of Common Prayer, we sang these remarkable words, which were taken by the good bishop (who loved a challenge) as the text of his sermon:

> The singers and trumpeters shall he rehearse:
> All my fresh springs shall be in thee.

God rehearsing his musicians! A poet finding the springs of his art in Zion! The words and images have played in my mind ever since.

In later years of study, I found that in the Psalms religion and the arts do indeed pulsate together. And so it seemed that a good way to present the Psalms would be to explore them along the paths of the various arts. This is what our book will attempt.

Painting and sculpture will not be treated directly, having little connection with the Psalms as originally used. But the chapters will take in turn the paths of poetry, architecture, music, dance and drama, and all will be found to lead to the heart of the Psalms. Discovered along these paths, the Psalms spring to life in all their passion and joy. And we may be left wanting to look afresh at religion and art today, having seen the vitality they gave each other in their youthful days of unity in the Psalms.

Introducing the Psalms
Almost everyone has heard or sung a psalm. Before many a

football cup final, at almost every funeral, Psalm 23, 'The Lord's my shepherd', rings out. Great national ceremonies, televised across the world, resound with Psalm 100, 'All people that on earth do dwell'. These and other psalms, translated as modern hymns, find constant use in churches and schools. Even if the chanting or reciting of entire psalms is not as common as it was, their influence is still pervasive. Through all the Church's centuries, they have been a daily food. Above all other books of the Bible, they have been able to partner the gospels, uncannily turning this later Christian message into song and worship.

One hundred and fifty pieces of Hebrew poetry make up the Book of Psalms, a collection grown from earlier collections. 'Psalm' means generally a song from worship with instrumental accompaniment; the word is found in the headings of many of these pieces, but the collection as a whole is known in Hebrew as the 'Praises'. Praise indeed prevails there, but only through a tremendous struggle with suffering. The struggle is expressed in many lamenting psalms, which lead the afflicted to throw themselves on God.

There is in fact much variety in these pieces. There are the tragic supplications and the jubilant praises and thanksgivings. There are voices of groups and of individuals. There are pieces portraying great ceremonies, with processions, massed assemblies, crowning of kings. There are oracles, where God speaks as through a prophet. All these and more varieties invite careful study, to sort them into types and to look for the different situations for which they were designed. Our chapters will explore all these matters.

The authorship of the Psalms will also be considered. King David came gradually to be credited with composing most of them, and his name already appears in the headings of seventy-three. But the part of the musical guilds at the temples will have to be noted, and credit given to their hereditary skill and dedication to music and poetry.

The land of the Psalms
The heartland of the people of these poems is in the mountains

which rise west of the River Jordan and the Dead Sea. The western slopes of these mountains receive good rains in winter and spring, but the eastern sides are dry and eroded by winds from the great deserts. Famous towns like Shechem, Jerusalem, Bethlehem and Hebron were strung along the watershed, and the people knew well the contrast of life and death in soil and climate. Even in the fertile regions the balance was precarious. The regular drought from May to October could sometimes be prolonged. Winters of poor rains meant starvation. Springs were few and water had to be carefully stored in cisterns. The Israelites themselves did not have much to do with the nearby Mediterranean coast. Their imagery of foaming waves and storms at sea probably draws on older poetry from the Lebanese coast.

The mountains and the fringe of desert areas gave some protection from invaders. But the strategic importance of the territory, as a bridge between Asia, Africa and Europe, meant that the intervals of peace were few.

All these conditions are mirrored in the Psalms. The grim and rocky contours of the desert, the high-soaring eagle, the shepherd whose task was so hard in the harsh wilderness, the lions, foxes, snakes, birds, mountain goats and rock badgers, the gullies that run and turn green for a short season – all are there. So also the hillsides that clap and sing for their rich yield of grain and figs, vines and olives, and yield the staff of bread, and wine that makes the heart merry and oil that makes the face shine. The enemies are there, armies that hack down the carved work of God's temple and slaughter young and old, enemies that trick and curse. And there are victories too, when the snares are broken, the cords loosed, prisoners freed, wounds healed, and 'peace', full life before God, abounds.

In such a land the people sang to God with passion. They wept for the rains and danced over the promise of them. They wailed and made imprecations against invaders and op-pressors. They danced and sang over God's gifts of freedom and healing.

3

The setting of the Psalms

Songs of worship were felt to be most appropriately sung in the nearer presence of God. His presence was symbolized at a sanctuary, as though it was his 'house', tended by his servants, the priests and similar orders. Daily sacrifices were offered to him in the courts with songs of prayer and praise. Individuals with special needs would come and pray, and psalms would be sung for them. The king especially, as chief steward of this household, would come with the burdens of his office, his frailties and dangers, to call upon God with offerings and psalms. The regular festivals saw people stream from far and near to take part for days on end in ceremonies which enthralled with music, dance and drama.

Once David had founded his dynasty (c.1000 BC), Jerusalem came to the fore as the chief centre of worship, and it is from the continuing worship at Jerusalem that the Psalms come. Some pieces may have travelled there from other sanctuaries, such as Hebron, Bethel, Dan, and Gilgal near Jericho. Dan, at the foot of the giant Mount Hermon and beside the bubbling sources of the Jordan, must have been a particularly inspiring place for the poets. Still, it is only Jerusalem (also called Zion) that is clearly named, and it was there that the main Israelite tradition of worship and psalm-singing survived into the Christian era.

One festival fell about March or April and eventually combined two observances: the night of Passover and the week of Unleavened Bread. The Passover commemorated the escape of the ancestors from Egypt; but only near the end of the monarchy did it develop from a custom in the home to a public gathering. Unleavened Bread was basically a celebration of the earliest harvest, barley. First cuttings and first-born animals would be offered to God, so that the rest could be thankfully put to human use. The ban on leaven would originally be to keep the new produce distinct from the old, but later it signified the haste of the meal in the Exodus.

The festival of Weeks (Pentecost) was counted seven weeks after Unleavened Bread. It was sometimes called Harvest, and it celebrated the wheat harvest. In much later times it was

4

linked with the founding of God's covenant with Israel.

But the festival most prominent in the narratives and most mirrored in the Psalms fell about September or October. There will have been an extended holy season, the forerunner of the present Jewish New Year, Atonement, and Tabernacles ('Ingathering' in older biblical texts). This autumn festal season had special urgency as being on the threshold of the rainy season, with the new cycle of growth at stake. The whole society therefore threw itself into prayer and praise; and ceremonies re-enacted the theme of creation, showing God as the victor over chaos, and lord of the life-yielding waters. 'The Lord is King!', went up the cry, and with trumpets, clapping and prostrations, and with dancing to all the instruments, they expressed their faith that he was lord of life.

It was a tremendous occasion. The hillsides around the fortress-city, covered with camps of the pilgrims, resounded with the psalms and acclamations. The sacred way up to the city and temple was the scene of exciting processions. The temple itself, with its bronze pillars and honey-coloured stone, gleamed on the summit in the fiery sun. And above all, the people participated with all their hearts.

The Psalms are the eloquent witness of all this. Here we shall meet, again and again, that enthusiasm in worship which rises to the final height, the ultimate Halleluia:

Every breathing thing, PRAISE THE LORD!

(150.6)

The Psalms in history

From its beginnings, the worshipping community sang to the Lord. Tradition told of the founder-members launching the songs – Miriam, prophetess and sister of Moses, leading the praise with hand-drum and dance (Exod. 15.20–21), and Moses himself singing with the congregation (Exod. 15; Deut. 32). In the centuries when the tribes lived in loose association (c.1200–1030), worship was their bond; great songs were raised, as when the prophetess Deborah celebrated the defeat of the armoured divisions of Sisera (Judg. 5).

5

From the followers of the first king, Saul, emerged an able leader, famous for his music. It was this David who first conquered Jerusalem for Israel (c.1000 BC) and made it the centre of his kingdom. With much dancing and music of praise, he installed there the ancient sacred symbol, the ark of the covenant, and thus gave the city a deep religious significance for Israel, which his son Solomon brought to full expression by building the splendid temple. Under these kings the forms of worship were duly ordered, and not least, the singing of psalms. Part of the tribes later split away as the Northern Kingdom, worshipping especially at Bethel and Dan, and in the eighth century were annexed into the Assyrian empire. But Jerusalem continued with its Davidic kings and temple until 586 BC. Then the Babylonians destroyed the temple and city, and carried the royal family and the leading classes into captivity. Guilds of psalm-singers, not parting from their lyres, sat mourning by the water-ways of Babylon (Ps. 137), but at the ruined temple, for some fifty years, a kind of lamenting worship continued. 'How long, how long, O God?' the singers urged (Ps. 74).

With the rise of the Persians to their two centuries of world empire, the temple could be rebuilt (515 BC), and those who could remember the first temple wept afresh (Ezra 3.12). When the city's defences were restored by the governor Nehemiah (c.444 BC), the psalmists took the lead in the dedication. Along the top of the walls they marched, one party circling round the north, the other round the south. They joined in the east and descended into the temple courts, where sacrifices were offered with singing and playing of instruments (Neh. 12.31f.), and the joy was heard far away. It may be at about this period that our collection of psalms was rounded off.

From 333 BC the Persians gave way to the Greeks. Through good times and bad the songs of the temple continued. Writing about 200 BC, Ben Sirah describes the scene on the Day of Atonement, when the high priest (who had inherited the trappings of the former kings) came forth 'like the morning star' from the inner sanctuary and made offerings at

6

the altar in the open court before the massed pilgrims. The priests blew trumpets, the people bowed low, the singers raised psalms and prayers (Ecclus. 50). Soon afterwards came a time of bitter persecution, when Antiochus IV forced the temple to fit with the imperial worship of Zeus (167–4 BC). The deaths of the martyrs gave impulse to the development of Jewish ideas of resurrection. The crisis passed, and for a while the Jews became more independent under rulers from a priestly family, the Hasmoneans or Maccabees, some of whom even took the title 'king'. Sects and monastic orders grew up in outlying places and sometimes expressed their faith in forms like the Psalms.

Palestine passed under Roman supervision (64 BC), and with their support Herod became king (40 BC). One of the greatest builders, he undertook a wonderful reconstruction of the temple and its whole area. At this great centre of pilgrimage and study, the priests and psalmists flourished. But it was razed to the ground in the war with the Romans (AD 70). The tradition of the Psalms was abruptly ended, and the guilds of psalmists disappeared. The synagogues, local congregations of Jews all over the world, were places for the reading and teaching of the books of scripture, not for the rites of sacrifices and psalm-singing. Of all the instruments, only the signalling ram's-horn was heard there.

But the Jews carefully preserved the text of the Psalms, even with musical rubrics which were no longer understood. And in the growing Christian Church the Psalms sprang to new life. In the fourth century, St Chrysostom relates that on all sorts of occasions the singing of the Psalms comes 'first, midst, and last'. Their music drew Augustine to the Church. They became to him what they have been to many generations, and he relates in his *Confessions* (ix. 4): 'How I addressed you, my God, in those psalms! How my love for you was kindled by them, how I burned to recite them, if I could, throughout the world to oppose the pride of mankind!' And out in the deserts, the hermit kept hold on his representative vocation through constant recital of the Psalms. Nothing, he believed, so exasperated the demons and Satan himself.

7

The Psalms and the nations

This love of the Psalms among the gentiles prompts thoughts about the 'chosen people' and the universal family. The Old Testament presents both themes strongly: the nations as the one family of Man (*adam*); and the sub-division, the children of Israel (or Jacob) who have a calling, with conditions and responsibilities, to be closest to the Lord.

The special calling is clearly expressed in the Psalms. 'He has not dealt so with any other nation' (147.20). 'In Judah God has made himself known' (76.1). The ruler of David's line is his chief servant, like an adopted son (2.7). And Jerusalem, Zion, is chief of the sanctuaries where God is revealed (87.1).

But the Psalms strikingly express the other theme too, the universal, as St Paul knew well (Rom. 15). Jerusalem is seen as the world-mother (Ps. 87). The Psalms aim to lead the worship of all on earth, every living being, and to resound in harmony with the praising music of the heavens (148; 150). Nations as allies of chaos are indeed seen as defeated, but nations as turned to God are to join in the singing and dance to his glory (Ps. 47).

The Psalms here match their origin, for they arose as Israelite faith united with poetic and musical traditions of the wider Near East. As the temple was built with the help of Phoenician architects, craftsmen and materials, so the musical guilds and learned schools of David and Solomon drew on the skills of older Palestinian culture and contacts with the civilizations of Egypt, Mesopotamia, Syria and beyond.

And now, miraculously, from the dust of thousands of years, the voices of these non-Israelite psalmists have come to be heard again in our times through the work of archaeologists, decipherists and linguists. From ancient Babylon we can hear again the thanksgiving of a healed man who walked the processional way to Babylon's temple and passed through the eleven gates which symbolized cleansing, new life, and joyful approach to the feet of the deity. He praises the Creator who can restore the dead to life: wherever the earth is founded and the heaven stretched out, wherever the sun shines and fire blazes, wherever water runs and wind blows, let the creatures of clay, blessed with life, sing the Creator's praise!

A vivid record of ancient Egyptian psalm-praise runs along the walls of the great colonnade in Luxor. For there the scenes of the Opet-festival are amply portrayed in relief, a combination of pictures and explanatory texts. Along one wall the outward procession is shown, scene by scene, as the divine symbols are taken by land and water to a neighbouring temple; the opposite wall gives the return journey. The scenes show parties of bearers and hauliers, lively dancers (Fig. 1), trumpeters, drummers, players of clackers, shakers and lutes, priests who sing and clap (Fig. 2). There are stations where sacrifices are offered, and inscriptions give the words of the hymns. Though the religious conceptions are in some ways very different from Israel's, one is reminded of David's procession with the ark (2 Sam. 6), especially regarding the sacrifices, dancing and music of praise.

From the wall of a tomb of the fourteenth century BC comes the most beautiful Egyptian hymn. It expresses the faith of the Pharaoh Akh-en-aton in the giver of life who appears in the sun-disk (the Aton). The deity is praised as filling every land with his beauty. At his daily rising men rise, wash and dress their bodies, and raise their arms to praise him; animals and plants rejoice, and birds stretch their wings in praise. As his rays shine into the green waters, ships on the Nile skim north and south and fish dart before his face. Already in the womb he is nurse to the child, stilling its crying. He gives breath to the chick in the shell and appoints it a time to come forth, speak, and walk upon its legs. How manifold the Creator's work! By him alone all live.

These few examples point, then, to the wider tradition of praise in the Near East, which goes back in fact to the earliest records. From the wider tradition came that of the Hebrew psalms, conscious of unique vocation, but still addressing the creator and his universal love. When the temple vanished, they spread more and more among the nations. Translated into all the tongues, they still lead the music of the world's prayer and praise.

Fig. 1 Nubian festal dancers

Fig. 2 Egyptian trumpeter and singing priests

10

2

POETRY AND THE PSALMS

Can poetry be translated?
Long ago, a collection of poetry was deprived of the music
with which it had been created and performed. It was handed
down for centuries in writing that took little note of vowels.
Eventually it was translated into quite alien languages, thereby
losing its own words, sounds and rhythms. It also lost
meaning through misunderstandings or obstacles of translation. In this impoverished form it was then circulated in a
world which could scarcely have understood the circumstances and aims of the original poets, so much had the
conditions of life changed. What hope had this material now of
moving hearts as great poetry should?

And yet the miracle happened. In many languages, in many
centuries and many societies, the Psalms have lived on, used
and loved perhaps more than any other poetry. Sometimes a
gifted translator played his part. One such was Coverdale
(1488–1569), worthy himself to carry the lyre. Many have
come to love his melodious version preserved in the Book of
Common Prayer. What magic is here:

> Though ye have lien among the pots,
> yet shall ye be as the wings of a dove,
> that is covered with silver wings,
> and her feathers like gold.

(68.13)

Or here:

> Like as the hart desireth the water-brooks,
> so longeth my soul after thee, O God.
>
> (42.1)

Another good example is his account of the prospering wicked:

> For they are in no peril of death
> but are lusty and strong.
> They come in no misfortune like other folk,
> neither are they plagued like other men.
> And this is the cause that they are so holden with pride
> and overwhelmed with cruelty.
> Their eyes swell with fatness
> and they do even what they lust.
> They corrupt other and speak of wicked blasphemy,
> their talking is against the most High.
> For they stretch forth their mouth unto the heaven
> and their tongue goeth through the world.
> Therefore fall the people unto them,
> and thereout suck they no small advantage.
> Tush, say they, how should God perceive it?
> Is there knowledge in the most High?
>
> (73.4–11)

And another of his memorable renderings:

> When the Lord turned again the captivity of Sion,
> then were we like unto them that dream.
> Then was our mouth filled with laughter
> and our tongue with joy.
>
> (126. 1–2)

Coverdale's success is to have matched qualities of the original. The melody and lilt of the words and the power of the images are achieved in a diction that is simple, direct and

12

without pretence. Any translation that respects these qualities seems to mediate the ancient vitality. Not himself a Hebraist, Coverdale had chiefly to work from a Latin translation of a Greek translation of the Hebrew, while profiting as he could from the more direct work of pioneers on the continent. But through his work the ancient poetry was to live again and fill the hearts and tongues of many generations.

Lines and metres

A patient consideration of the system of Hebrew poetry is rewarding. For poetry is speech that is dancing and, no less than the skilful dance, rests on a discipline of patterns and rhythms.

Hebrew poetry falls into recognizable 'lines', which consist usually of two parts or 'members', sometimes of three. The statements usually flow in short clauses identical with these lines or their members. Here is an example, with the second member of each 'line' indented:

> He sent before them a man,
>   for a slave was Joseph sold.
> They afflicted his feet with fetters,
>   his neck came into the irons.
> Till his prediction came true,
>   the word of the Lord refined him.
> The king sent and released him,
>   the ruler of peoples, yes, he freed him.
> He made him lord of his house
>   and ruler of all his estate,
> to bind his princes at his wish
>   and teach his elders wisdom.

(105.17–22)

The structure is thus clear and fairly symmetrical, though the lines and members cannot be shown to conform to exact measurements of words or syllables. In pursuit of such measurements, some scholars examine the varieties of Hebrew poetry by rigorous counting of syllables per line and member

13

in order to obtain at least an accurate preliminary description. This procedure throws little light on the poetic quality of the material; in view of the rather varied totals thus obtained, it is unlikely that the poets thought in terms of fixed numbers of syllables or words.

The counting of the chief stresses (usually one on each word or word-group) is more revealing, bringing out the rhythm of the poetry and so its connection with music and dance. Thus a line may have two members in each of which there seem to be three stresses. We can mirror it roughly in English, our hyphened phrases representing one Hebrew word or word-group:

> Mágnify the-Lórd with-mé,
> let-us-exált his-náme togéther!
> I-soúght the-Lórd and-he-ánswered-me
> and-from-áll my-térrors he-sáved-me.

> (34.3–4)

This rhythmic pattern is the commonest and is referred to by scholars as 3+3.

A special eloquence belongs to the rhythm described as 3+2, where the second member has only two stresses. This early falling away, perhaps originally matching a dance-step, has a pathetic, elegiac effect and was favoured for laments, though it is found more widely:

> The-Lórd is-my-líght and-my-salvátion, –
> whóm shall-I-féar?
> The-Lórd is-the-stréngth of-my-life, –
> at-whóm shall-I-trémble?

> (27.1)

Members with only two stresses sometimes follow each other, and Psalm 43 begins with a series of such short members:

14

Júdge-for-me, Gód,
    and-conténd in-my-caúse
against-a-peóple dislóyal,
    from-mén of-decéit
    and-iniquity deliver-me!

(43.1)

Members with four stresses occur:

But-ráther in-the-teáching of-the-Lórd is-his-pleásure,
    from-his-teáching he-chánts by-dáy and-by-níght.

˙ (1.2)

There is considerable freedom in the arrangement of these
rhythmic patterns, and scarcely two psalms are alike. For
example, we can take two neighbouring psalms. Psalm 13 has
lines with stresses as follows: 4+4, 4+3+4, 4+4; 4+3;
3+3+4. Psalm 14, however, yields the following: 3+2; 3+2;
3+2, 3+2; 2+2; 2+2; 3+3+2; 3+2; 3+2; 4+4+4. There is
also much difference in the number of lines, ranging between
the shortest, Psalm 117, with two lines, and the longest, Psalm
119, with one hundred and seventy six.

Stanzas and alphabetic psalms
There is also much freedom in the length of sections within a
psalm, so that one can rarely make out anything as precise as
the stanzas of European poetry. In Psalm 99, for example, a
varied refrain praising God's holiness comes at the end of
verses 3, 5, and 9, but the sections thus marked off are all of
different pattern. A few psalms are constrained by being
acrostics, each line (or member, or group of lines) beginning
with the next letter of the alphabet (Pss. 9–10; 25; 34; 37; 111;
112; 119; 145), but this constraint still allowed freedom in the
measure of the line. The alphabetic form was useful as an aid
to memory, but was probably valued also for its sense of
completeness and its mystical force. Only Psalm 119 goes to
the length of having for each letter a section of eight lines

15

which each begin with that letter, and which use in turn one of the eight terms denoting the teaching of the Lord (law, commandments, precepts, words etc.). The translator needs some freedom to imitate this effect; here is an attempt at the section beginning with the letter P:

> Promises from you are marvellous,
>   so I guard them with my life.
> Putting forth meaning, your word gives light,
>   making wise the simple.
> Panting with open lips I thirst
>   and long for your commands.
> Peace be on me from your merciful face,
>   after your rule for lovers of your name!
> Plant my feet right by your speaking to me
>   and let no evil take power over me!
> Preserve me from man's oppression
>   that I may keep your principles!
> Pour light from your face on your servant
>   and teach me your decrees!
> Plashing waters, my tears drop down
>   that men have not kept your teaching.
>
> (119.129–136)

Word-music

Repetition of particular consonants occurs also as part of the word-music of the Hebrew phrases. Most of this, and especially the characteristic guttural and emphatic consonants, must be lost or transformed in translation. What liquid melody runs through this blessing of 'the City of Peace', that is, 'Jerusalem'! –

> *sha-alu sha-lom yeru-sha-lem*
>   *yish-la-yu oha-bayik*
> *yehi sha-lom behe-lek*
>   *shal-wa be-ar-meno-tayik*

16

Pray for the peace of Jerusalem!
  Tranquil be those who love you!
Peace be within your wall,
  in your palaces all tranquillity!

(122.6–7)

While there is here a deliberate play on the words for 'peace'
and 'tranquillity', prompted by the very name 'Jerusalem', in
many cases the poet's instinct led him naturally to a music of
word-sounds:

lu-le yah-we sheha-ya la-nu
  yo-mar-na yis-ra-el
lu-le yah-we sheha-ya la-nu
  bequm a-ley-nu a-dam. . .
If the Lord had not fought for us,
  let Israel now declare,
if the Lord had not fought for us,
  when men leapt out upon us. . .

(124.1f)

The resonance of the consonant 'm' comes in readily, as
Hebrew uses it in several ways for forming and modifying
words:

miq-qo-lot ma-yim rab-bim
  ad-di-rim mish-berey yam
ad-dir bam-ma-rom yah-we
Over the tumult of the Mighty Ones the Waters,
  their Majesties the Breakers of the Sea,
prevailed in majesty the Master on high.

(93.4)

Rhy.nes were not part of the poetic system and only occur
occasionally as part of the general melody of wording:

nenat-teka et mo-sero-temo
wenash-li-ka mim-men-nu abo-temo

17

Let us snap the bonds-of-them,
  throw off from us the cords-of-them!

(2.3)

The art of parallelism

So far we have considered the poetry of the Psalms in terms of
its sounds, – the length, composition and rhythm of its lines
and the music of its consonants and vowels. In favour of the
translator here were the freedom and variety of the measures,
the simplicity of the syntax, the directness of expression. The
translator can try to match these qualities in his own language,
even if the lilt and melody of his own word-sounds must be
different from those of the Hebrew.

But we still have to consider the most celebrated feature of
Hebrew poetry, a feature which fortunately can be well
represented in translation. This is known as 'parallelism', a
balanced construction in which one line or member repeats the
meaning or form of the other. Sometimes the correspondence
is complete ('synonymous') – every word has its counterpart:

The-Lord has-heard my-supplication,
  the-Lord accepts my-prayer.

(6.9)

In another kind, the correspondence may lie in a comparison
('emblematic'):

As the father loves his children,
  the Lord loves his fearers.

(103.13)

Or again, a contrast may be used ('antithetic'), as when justice
is affirmed in its two aspects:

The wicked must borrow and cannot repay,
  but the righteous give alms liberally,
for those blessed by him shall inherit the earth,
  and those cursed by him shall be cut off.

(37.21–2)

18

Quite often the balance is only in the form of rhythm, not in repetition of sense. In this kind (called 'formal' or 'synthetic') the statement moves on more swiftly:

> Blessed be the Lord!
>> With miracles he stood by me
>>> in a city under siege.
> And I in my panic had said,
>> I am cut off from before your eyes!
> But you heard
>> the noise of my entreaties
>>> when I cried out to you.

(31.21–2)

Repetition of meaning is often used incompletely, – the following line or member repeats part of the preceding:

> Save my soul from the sword,
>> my precious from the grip of the dog!

(22.20)

With such partial repetition there may be added a new element:

> Give to the Lord, you company of heaven,
>> give to the Lord the glory and power!

(29.1)

In this example the extra element in the second member was necessary to the sense of the first. So the first is in suspense till the second resolves it at the end, as in this further example:

> For look, your enemies, Lord,
>> for look, your enemies perish!

(92.9)

The device can have a hovering, darting motion, turning a simple statement into a fascinating disclosure. The outstanding example lies outside the Psalms:

> Between her feet he bowed, he fell, he lay,
>> between her feet he bowed, he fell.
> Where he bowed,
>> there he fell, shattered.

(Judg.5.27)

This ancient style appears in some psalms:

> The voice of the Lord with strength,
>> the voice of the Lord with majesty,
> the voice of the Lord breaking cedars, –
>> then the Lord broke down cedars of Lebanon.

(29.4–5)

> Mountain of God, mountain of Bashan,
>> many-peaked mountain, mountain of Bashan,
> why do you envy, many-headed mountain,
>> the mountain God wants for his dwelling,
>> where the Lord will abide for ever?

(68.15–16)

Advantages of parallelism
Although examples can be culled of one or another variety of parallelism, any complete psalm will usually present its own pattern, rich in peculiar variations. It seems that the poets, familiar with the basic method, were able to vary it for their own purposes in innumerable ways. The balancing patterns could be extended from the parts of a line to a series of lines (Ps.124). The effect of the balance was always beauty, and then, as required, pathos, suspense, climax, and emphasis of sorrow or joy. The short clauses help each other, looking at the matter from different angles, adding detail and clarification, and all without losing the simple syntax:

20

I waited, waited for the Lord
    and he bent to me and heard my crying,
and he brought me up from the raging pit,
    from the miry swamp,
and he set my feet on a rock,
    making my steps firm,
and he put in my mouth a new song,
    a hymn to our God.
Many saw and feared
    and trusted in the Lord.

(40.1–3)

The wording of Hebrew poetry can thus remain lean. Not only in the simplicity of construction, but also in the sparsity of adjectives there is a contrast with much English verse. By way of illustration, here is a close translation of Psalm 23:

The Lord (being) my shepherd, I do not lack,
    in fields of grass he lets me lie,
by waters of rest he leads me,
    he restores my soul,
he guides me in roads of right
    for the sake of his name. . .

In contrast, the hymn of Joseph Addison:

When in the sultry glebe I faint
or on the thirsty mountain pant,
to fertile vales and dewy meads
my weary wandering steps he leads,
where peaceful rivers, soft and slow,
amid the verdant landscape flow.

In translation we often have to use an adjective where the Hebrew uses linked nouns in a very flexible construction: for 'waters of rest' we render 'still waters' or 'refreshing waters'; for 'mountain of his holiness' we render 'his holy mountain'. The translation often needs to add an adjective to clarify the bare noun of the Hebrew, and so we render a single word as 'sure defence', 'burnt offerings', 'fatherless children', 'wonderful works', 'saving power', 'wild oxen', 'joyous song', 'steadfast love'.

Favourite pairs and families of words

The use of parallel statements, balancing, echoing or filling out each other, means that certain words will be matched together in the corresponding clauses fairly regularly. In addition to words that are commonly thus paired, there grow little families of words, revolving round a common theme and offering themselves readily to the poet as he moved through his pattern of balancing statements. Thus, around the theme of God's covenant or bond, and all the trustworthy, enduring care with which he maintains it, we have such words as:

hesed	fidelity (KJ: mercy, RSV: steadfast love)
emet	truth, steadfastness
emuna	faithfulness
rahamim	compassion, love
sedeq	right, good order (KJ: righteousness)
mishpat	good rule, justice
shalom	peace, health, plenty
tob	goodness, provision
yeshu-a	salvation

With such words, the goodness and good acts of God as caring lord of his people and world are praised, not least when he is to be urged to manifest them by worshippers who feel forgotten or forsaken:

> I will always sing of the Lord's acts of fidelity,
>   for ever I will make known your faithfulness with
> my mouth,
> I declare your fidelity is built high,
>   you have established your faithfulness into the
> heavens,
> (saying) 'I have made a bond with my chosen one,
>   I have sworn to David my servant. . .'
> Order and justice are supports of your throne,
>   fidelity and truth go before your face.

(89.1–3,14)

The good values there are seen as angels attending the Lord. Here they are again, delightfully active in a vision of a good year to come:

> Fidelity and Truth have embraced,
>> Order and Plenty have kissed each other,
> Truth sprouts from the earth,
>> Order leans out from heaven's window,
> yes, the Lord will give Goodness
>> and our land will give its yield,
> Order will march before him
>> and prepare in the way for his steps.
>>
>> (85.10–13)

Obviously, the study of words and their meanings should take account of such pairings and families, which sometimes have a history reaching back to earlier peoples.

Poetic images

In considering the poetic imagery of the Psalms, we have to reckon with a poetic view of the world and of all man's experience. While there is no elaborate mythology, like that inherited by European poetry with numerous names and adventures of gods and spirits, there is more poetry than science in the understanding of the universe, Creator and creatures.

The act of creation was seen in colourful terms, – it follows the Creator's battle with monsters and waters that represent chaos:

> It was you who split the sea in your might,
>> you broke the heads of the dragons on the waters.
>>
>> (74.13)

The upper part of the sundered sea was now made into a heavenly ocean, in and above which God build his palace and throne (29.10). God himself is robed in light, and makes the clouds his chariot and rides on the wings of the wind (104.1–

23

4). While our modern calculations of the size of the universe may be in danger of stunning the imagination, homely images in the Psalms reach down to our minds without losing the wonder:

He gathered as in a bottle the waters of the sea,
  putting the deeps in storehouses.

(33.7)

In heaven is the divine company: the holy ones, the angels, the cherubim. They meet in council (82; 89.5). On a cherub, too, part animal in form and winged, the Lord may ride down to snatch the sufferer from the jaws of death (18.10).

The Creator has spread out the heavens like a wide bedouin tent, to be a canopy over the earth, but also a firm vault upholding the ocean, stores and dwellings of the heavenly region. In this 'firmament' he has set sun and moon, also the stars which, for all their myriads, he counts exactly and names one by one (147.4).

All lives. The firmament and the day and night sing the Creator's praise (19.1f). Dawn is awakened by music of praise (57.8) and sweeps across the skies on her wings (139.9); from her womb is born, glistening with dew, the Lord's royal priest and champion (110.3). The sun appears radiant, like a bridegroom from his wedding-bower, and rejoices to run his track like a hero (19.4–6).

Between its 'ends' the earth has great width (110.6; 48.10). The Creator drove the lower part of the primeval waters off its surface and fixed it in those waters with mountain-pillars (104.5f.; 24.2; 46.2; 75.3), cleaving passages for sweet waters to spring and gush (104.10f.; 74.15). Descent into the earth at death leads through the underlying waters to Sheol, the land of the dead. In extremes of suffering, one seems to enter its gates (9.13), to sink into its miry mouth (69.1–2,15; 40.2). The sufferer, sinking towards death, thus cries 'from the ends of the earth', from the cataracts and breakers (42.7), from the depths (130.1), from the pit (88.6), from the traps of hunter death (18.4–5). No depth, no darkness can bar the saviour's way.

24

He can strike through the ocean depths, through the world's foundations (18.15), and shatter the prison doors (107 16)

The earth and sea are filled with a teeming life which all belongs to the Lord and is in his care (24.1; 104.24). Many creatures are observed keenly, like the lions which roar in the night in request of food from God (104.21) or the baby ravens cawing in their nests (147.9), while a certain mystery covers the things innumerable, small and great, that live in the sea (104.25) and make their way along its tracks (8.8). We hear of the dove that flies into the remote wilderness (55.5f.), the swallow nesting at the temple (84.3), the eagle or griffon vulture which renews its plumage (103.5), the solitary owl and perhaps pelican (102.6), the wild goats and badgers in their rocky refuges (104.18), the bees angrily swarming (118.12), the nesting stork (104.17), wild asses or zebras (104.11), fallow deer that snuff for scent of water (42.1), the war-horse, proud and strong (20.7; 32.9; 147.10), the flimsy locust (109.23), the despised worm (22.6), the wild dogs or jackals that creep into the town at night, eerily howling (59.6f.). Death's demons have bestial forms – packs of dogs, lions, huge bulls, serpent and dragon (22.16f.; 91.13). The flock of sheep and goats is a favourite image, creatures harmless, vulnerable, happy with a good shepherd, grazing, drinking, lying, skipping (23; 44.11; 80.1; 100.3, 114.6).

Then there are images of the family: the father tender-hearted to his children (103.13), assisting at their birth (22.9–10); the mother in travail (48.6) or nursing her baby at her breast (22.9), comforting her weaned child (131.2), busy in the inmost home, her children round the meal-table like lively olive-slips shooting up around the old tree (128.3); brothers, a strength to reckon with and a pleasant fellowship (127.5; 133.1). The bridegroom has his moment of glory (19.5) and the bride her beauty (45.13). There are the fatherless and widows, the solitary, the broken-hearted, the homeless, the prisoners, the hungry, the blind, the deaf; for such are the miracles of God (38.13; 68.5–6; 113.9; 146.7f.; 147.2f.).

Images arise also from work, – the refiner (12.6), the rapid scribe (45.1), the builder (127.1), the watchman (130.6), the

25

hunter and the fowler (7.15; 56.6; 124.7), the snake-charmer (58.5), the tenders of vines (80.8f.), olives (52.8; 128.3) and other trees (1.3), the ploughman (129.3) and the winnower (1.4). We notice also the skin bottles stored under the smoky roof (119.83). How harmful are malevolent words – like a razor, a sword, or an arrow (52.2; 64.3)! The traitor's speech is like butter and oil, soft and smooth, but he hides a drawn sword (55.21).

There are many images from the elements, from the field and wilderness. Volcano, earthquake and storm speak of the terribleness of God (18.7f.; 29.3–8; 97.3; 104.32). His wonders are seen in snow that covers like wool, hoarfrost which he scatters like wood-ash, icy hail-stones, frozen waters (147.16– 18). More characteristic is the hot wind across the desert which soon withers the wild spring flowers and verdure (11.6; 103.15–16). For journeys through the great, harsh distances of the mountainous wilderness, how essential to know the path (1.6; 2.12; 16.11; 107.7, 40), how welcome a spring (105.41)!

The quickly-passing flowers of Palestine's spring are an image of man's transience (37.2; 90.5–6), as also is the evening shadow in that land of little twilight (102.11; 109.23), the fading dream (73.20; 90.5), the worn garments which could not be so easily replaced, and the fretting of the moth (102.26; 39.11). But the renewal of life also seizes attention: the parched torrent-beds of the Negev suddenly come to life; the winter waters pour down them and borders of living green envelop them (126.4). The cliffs and crags of the wilderness appear again and again, places to fall, or by God's help to tread surely, places of refuge, strongholds (27.5; 40.2; 73.18), images of God himself (18.2,31; 28.1; 71.3).

The imagery of fellowship with God
The spell of the Psalms as poetry lies above all in one prevailing application of their poetic genius, the portrayal of fellowship with God. We have seen how the dreadfulness of God was depicted with the colours of storm, fire, earthquake and volcano. Awe is evoked also in the contemplation of his multitudinous works, great and small:

When I look at your heavens
   things made by your fingers,
    the moon and the stars you have set there, –
what is man that you remember him,
   the son of man that you care for him?

(8.3–4)

What fingers! And what skill, what wisdom in them! –

Lord, how many things you have made,
   and all of them shaped with wisdom!

(104.24)

Here we see the genius of this poetry of faith, – to convey the dread mystery of the Almighty through childlike images. Before we deride the human forms of this presentation of God, we may wonder whether any other terms have fostered knowledge of God as these have done. As in all Hebrew tradition, the boldness is breath-taking, but the power is undeniable:

Arouse yourself! Why are you sleeping, Lord?
   Awake! Do not spurn us!

(44.23)

Then the Lord like a sleeper woke up,
   like a mighty man sobering from wine,
and he struck his enemies backwards,
   made them a mockery for ever.

(78.65–6)

For such bold and colourful images of God we can compare a memorable passage in Psalm 60. To a people whose world seemed to be cracking under their feet, assurance is given through a vision of a God who declares his sovereignty over all their borders: over the town-holdings of Shechem west of the Jordan and Succoth on the east, over the tribal lands of Gilead, Manasseh and Ephraim. Honoured indeed is the leading tribe of Ephraim, royal is Judah, David's tribe; they shall be God's

27

helmet and sceptre. In subjugation is the easterly people of Moab; they are to be God's washbasin, a figure perhaps suggested by the view from Palestine's heights of the rim of Moabite mountains enclosing the bright blue waters of the Dead Sea. Southerly Edom too will be taken into possession, and God's shoe thrown over the property in legal gesture. On the west the Philistine coast is also a conquest, over which God will sing his song of victory:

> God speaks in his sanctuary:
> 'I will go up and share out Shechem
>   and measure the vale of Succoth.
> Mine shall be Gilead and mine Manasseh,
>   Ephraim the helmet of my head,
> Judah my sceptre,
>   Moab the pot I wash in,
> over Edom I will throw my sandal,
>   over Philistia I will shout victory.'

(60.6–8)

In similar manner we hear of God's laughing (2.4), fuming (74.1), marching with great steps (74.3), covering with his wings (57.1), scanning with his eyes (11.4), hearing with his ears (18.6; 130.2). Child-like, the suppliant cries loudly the better to be heard (142.1), and describes his sufferings volubly to stir God's compassion, and argues from God's own interest to move him to intervene. Childlike – and yet it is a poetry we can enter into with passion:

> You have counted the shakings of my head.
>   Put my tears in your bottle!
> Are they not numbered in your book?

(56.8)

> Pity me, Lord, in my distress!
>   My eye is wasted by trouble,
>   my soul also, and my belly.
> My life is used up with grieving,
>   my years with groaning.

My strength fails through my affliction
    and my bones are wasting away.
I am jeered at by all my opponents,
    I am become a horror to my neighbours and friends,
seeing me in the street, they flee from me,
    I am forgotten like one who has died,
    discarded like a broken pot.
I hear the whisperings of many,
    a terror on every side,
as they plot together against me,
    planning to take my life.
Yet I rely on you, Lord!
    I say, You are my God!
My times are in your hand; save me
    from the hand of my foes and pursuers!
May your face beam on your servant,
    deliver me by your fidelity!

(31.9–16)

Here is a God who holds our right hand; he is like a rock to us; he is our 'portion', a share of land from which we live. All this expresses his loving nearness and total sufficiency:

My heart was growing bitter,
    I felt a gnawing in my kidneys,
for I was stupid and could not understand,
    I was like a beast towards you.
But now I am ever beside you,
    you hold me by my right hand,
by your counsel you guide me,
    and at last you will take me into glory.
Whom do I need in heaven?
    Besides you I want no one on earth.
My heart and my flesh are spent, –
    rock of my heart and my portion is God for ever!

(73.21–6)

All needs gather into the one need, – to see the beauty of God,

and for this the image of thirst is often used, consuming thirst
in a dry wilderness:

> Lord, you are my God,
>   I search for you with longing.
> My soul thirsts for you,
>   my flesh yearns for you
> in a land of drought,
>   weary and waterless.
> So in the holy place I watch for you
>   to see your power and glory.
>
> (63.1–2)

To see his beauty is to find the fresh springs that restore to life,
to see the light in which the world of life rejoices:

> Beside you rises the spring of life,
>   in your light we see light.
>
> (36.9)

The tiny reflection in one's eye of a person standing close
suggests how that person has entered one's affections and
become tenderly cherished. So before the eye of God, the
believer finds entry into his heart; or again, he will nestle as a
young bird under the parent's wing:

> Keep me like the little one in your eye,
>   hide me in the shadow of your wings!...
> Through your goodness I shall behold your face;
>   awakening, I shall be satisfied by your form.
>
> (17.8,15)

Among such poetic expressions of encounter with God, Psalm
139 is outstanding. Assailed by cruel foes, the supplicant seeks
God's power against them, seeing them as enemies also of
God. But he knows that if he seeks God's help he must expose
his heart to God's searching. Before the prayer for help,

therefore, there is a long preparation in which he praises his Creator as able to know him through and through:

> Lord, you have searched me and known me,
>   you know my sitting down and my rising,
>   you understand my thought from afar,
> my journeys and my halts you know exactly,
>   you are familiar with all my ways.
> If there is a word on my tongue,
>   Lord, you know it entirely.
> Behind and before you close me about,
>   the palm of your hand is upon me.
> Such knowing is too wonderful for me,
>   too high for me to reach.
> Where could I go from your Spirit,
>   where could I flee from your face?
> If I go up to heaven, you are there,
>   if I spread my couch in the underworld, there you are!
> If I take the wings of dawn
>   and dwell in the far west of the sea,
> even there your hand will take me,
>   your right hand hold me.
> And if I say, Let darkness cover me,
>   and let the light become night about me,
> no darkness is too dark for you
>   and night becomes light as the day. . .
> For you have fashioned my kidneys,
>   you wove me in the womb of my mother.
> I praise you and tremble that I am so wonderfully made.
>   Your works are wonderful.
> How well you know my being!
>   my frame was not hidden from you
> when I was made in secret,
>   woven as in depths of the earth,
> your eyes saw my embryo,
>   and in your book days were written,
> all my days that were planned
>   before there was one of them.

How weighty your thoughts are for me,
  Lord, how vast the sum of them!
I count them, – they outnumber the sand-grains!
  I finish, – and there you are, still before me!

                            (139.1–18)

The forms of the psalms

Our consideration of the poetry of the Psalms began with attention to the forms of the lines – questions of measure and rhythm, balance and pattern. As regards their measurements, the forms of complete psalms appeared rather diverse and free.

However, these forms of complete psalms begin to fall into families when we recognize the traditional elements of thought from which they are built. Such an element may be worded in various ways, often with a fresh turn amidst the stereotyped expressions, but its main point remains. These elements are put together like building blocks according to the purpose of the psalm. Psalms of similar purpose thus have a similar structure of thought-elements ('motifs') and can be grouped together as a class.

Elements expressing praise

As an example of such elements of thought used as building blocks, we may take *the call to praise*. Parties are called upon to praise God; there is much interesting variety, but the thrust is the same:

Praise the Lord, all you nations!
  Glorify him, all you peoples!

                            (117.1)

Praise, you servants of the Lord,
  praise the name of the Lord!

                            (113.1)

My soul, bless the Lord,
  all my inner parts, bless his holy name!

                            (103.1)

With this is usually joined *the reason for the praise*. This element is often introduced with 'for':

> For his fidelity is mighty over us,
> and always the Lord proves true.

(117.2)

Or it may take the form of descriptive phrases:

> the forgiver of all your wickedness,
> the healer of all your sicknesses. . .

(103.3)

The two elements mentioned so far, the call to praise and the reason for praise, were sufficient for the construction of whole psalms. With variations, extensions and resumptions, they were built into fine exciting poems (such as Pss.147, 148 and 150) which are basic examples of the class we may call hymns or songs of praise. The aim of such psalms, as these elements make clear, is to lead the worshippers in acknowledgement and experience of God. In the nature of the case – the address being chiefly to the worshippers – God is most often referred to in the third person. When he is directly addressed in praise, favourite elements are the exclamation (8.1; 104.24) and the rhetorical question (89.8).

Related to these hymnic materials are other elements which treat the praise of God from rather special angles. Psalms which use them may be grouped as sub-divisions of the hymns or as related classes.

One such element is *the proclamation of God's reign* as an event, a new era. The characteristic formula is 'The Lord is King!' or, as we may translate, 'The Lord has become King!' The whole psalm reverberates with the excitement of the proclamation; so Psalms 47, 93, 96–99, and, a little differently, 29. The associated elements are calls to acknowledge this event and to tell it out across the world. We may also find here an element of *narrative depicting the Lord's victory* that has established his supremacy; thus Psalm 93.3–4, – the chaos waters surged high in royal pretensions, but the Lord proved to be their master. These psalms are often referred to as the Enthronement Psalms but it would be less confusing to call them Proclamations of God's kingship.

Another element related to the hymnic materials is *the appreciation of Jerusalem (Zion) or the temple*. City or sanctuary is praised as the abode of God and hence the place of refreshment in his grace and life. There are some half-dozen psalms where this element seems to give the theme for the whole psalm and these are sometimes treated as a class and called Songs of Zion (46, 48, 76, 84, 87, 122), though they differ in their patterns and immediate purpose. In three there is the element of narrative depicting the Lord's victory, here in defence of the city (46.6f.; 48.3f; 76.3f.); it may be that the reference is to a symbolic action showing the Lord's will to defend his city. Emphasizing the Lord's powerful presence, this element thus offers grounds for the appreciation of Zion. In two psalms there are references to the experience of pilgrimage to Zion (84.2f.; 122.1f.). We meet also the element of *benediction*: happy are those who can be in God's house (84.4f), prosperity to those who love his city (122)! – all indirect praise of God himself.

In a number of psalms similar to the hymns there is an element of *story relating a recent experience of salvation*. Usually combined with calls to praise, this story is an acknowledgement which sets the tone of the psalm as a thanksgiving; it may also turn to men in testimony. The story may describe the need, the prayer that had been offered, and God's gracious response. Such accounts of deliverance may come from the community (66.10–12; 124; 129), but more often from an individual (18.4f.; 30.1f.; 32.3f.; 116.1f.). Scholars therefore sometimes classify such psalms as Thanksgivings of the Community and Thanksgivings of the Individual. It seems that such types, in origin at least, would have accompanied *fulfilment of sacrificial vows* in thanksgiving at the temple, and we sometimes meet an element mentioning this (66.13–15; 116.17–18).

Elements for prayer

Of quite another mood are those which are used in anguished supplications, in 'laments' of community or individual. As an introduction we find *the plea for a hearing*, directly addressing God with his name 'Yahweh' (English translations usually 'Lord') and beseeching him to give ear to the prayer (130.1–2; 141.1; 143.1). The climax is provided by the element of *the petition* itself, praying for help or for the overthrow of oppressors (143.9–12; 142.6b; 141.9,10). In addition to the prayer using an imperative (e.g. 'Hear, Lord! Guard me! Arise, Lord!' Ps.17), there are wishes similar to *blessings* and *curses*: 'The Lord cut off all smooth-talking lips!' (12.3); 'May they be like chaff before the wind, the angel of the Lord driving them!' (35.5); 'May those who wish my good sing and rejoice. . .' (35.27). Occasionally the element of curse is used extensively, while still controlled by the consciousness that the issue must be in God's hands; the context is prayer, not curse-magic, though the imagery is heaped up and filled with all the poet's power (58.7f.; 69.22f.; 109.6f.).

Other elements serve to prepare for or reinforce the petitions. Chief of these is *the account of the suffering* (sometimes itself called 'the lament'), which is extremely pathetic as it seeks to move God's concern (42.3–4; 6.6–7; 22.11f.). Connected with this we often find the *sharp, appealing question*, asking *when* God will come (101.2), *how long* must the anguish continue (74.10), *why* does he not intervene (74.1). The prayer may also be reinforced by a *statement of trust*; in affirming his reliance on God (142.5), the suppliant would move the divine faithfulness (143.8,11,12). Related to this is *the assurance of having been heard*; the suppliant gains confidence that God has accepted him (6.8–10; 56.9f.; 54.4–5). This is sometimes followed by *the vow to give thanks with an offering* (54.6; 56.12) *or with a psalm* (7.17; 27.6; 13.6).

Elements of divine speech

Psalms of various types may contain an element of *oracle*, where the Lord speaks in the first person ('Be still and know that I am God' 46.10). The experience of poetry as 'inspired' is

35

here most direct. As a prophet or seer, the psalm-singer conveys words as heard from God and, as in the prophetic books, the divine speech flows in poetic form with striking imagery and strong turns of phrase. The situations of worship at the temple are usually evident. The poet may mediate God's word when God confronts the great assembly in renewal of his covenant (81.5f.). Or he may declare God's will at the installation of a king (110.1). The striving of the lamenting psalms for a response from God will often have been answered by an oracle, and occasionally this has been preserved for us (12.5; 60.6).

Elements of wisdom
There are some elements in the Psalms which give instruction not in the form of oracles but of 'wisdom', – in the manner of wise men, the respected sages and teachers, a style developed in the Near East from ancient times. A basic element here is the short *proverb*, as in this favourite kind where a comparison is set up, riddle-like, in the first part, and explained only in the second part:

> Like arrows in the hand of a mighty man –
> > so the sons of one's youth.
>
> (127.4)

Another element of teaching is *the pronouncement of happiness*:

> Happy the man who fears the Lord,
> > who delights greatly in his commandments!
>
> (112.1)

The manner of the fatherly sage is evident in the calls to his 'sons' or pupils to pay heed:

> Come, sons, listen to me!
> > In the fear of the Lord I will train you.
>
> (34.11)

36

The teaching concerns the greatest issues of life and right and is not without awe and mystery; it is 'wisdom', 'discernment,' 'parable', 'dark sayings' (49.3–4). Its favourite subjects are the contrasting destinies of the good person and the bad, the faith needed to endure the contradictions of experience, the cultivation of the fear of the Lord.

Classes of psalms

We have now surveyed most of the elements, the 'motifs', with which the psalms are constructed. Here is solid ground for understanding the purpose of a psalm and following the movement of its thought. It was apparent also that psalms with similar patterns of elements can be grouped in classes. The groupings that were proposed by the great pioneer of this approach, Hermann Gunkel (1862–1932), are as good as any, provided that they are regarded only as a useful preliminary to ordered study. Such classifications do not have authority enough to regulate the interpretation of particular psalms.

In this spirit, then, we can gather up our observations about types of psalms. It is useful to group together the psalms of praise, the *Hymns*, with their calls to praise and reasons for praise. We found a related group in the *Proclamations of God's kingship*, with their announcements of his ascension, accounts of his triumph and calls to acknowledge him and spread the good news. Another kindred group we found in the *Songs of Zion*, with their appreciation of Zion as the divine abode where he confounds assailants and receives pilgrims with gifts of life. The mood of praise led us also to the *thanksgivings*, with their praises and acknowledgements and fulfilment of vows occasioned by stories of recent salvation. Through such stories it may be seen whether the deliverance is of the people or of an individual, and we may usefully divide these psalms into *Thanksgivings of the Community* and *Thanksgivings of the Individual*.

The patterns of the prayers in distress showed considerable regularity, and since the supplicants portray themselves in their needs, we may again work with a distinction of people and individual, grouping these psalms as *Laments of the*

Community and the numerous *Laments of the Individual*. In both kinds one notices the bold, direct calling upon God, the pleas for a hearing and for speedy rescue, the moving depictions of danger and anguish, the sharp, appealing 'Why?' and 'How long?', the professions of trust, and sometimes the achievement of confidence and the vows to present psalms and offerings.

With other important elements it was not so easy to recognize patterns yielding major groupings. An oracle might form the main part of a psalm, but there were various situations in worship where such speeches of God might be presented, and so various combinations of elements. Again, with wisdom teachings, a few psalms, like Psalm 37, may be fatherly admonitions throughout, but the elements of proverb, pronouncements of happiness, comparisons and parables may also be used in other kinds of psalms.

We even have to take account of combinations of almost contradictory elements, as when elements of praise precede lament (27; 40; 89) or follow it (22; 69), or are interspersed with it (9–10; 102). Rather diverse elements also are combined in psalms that went with processional movements and interchanging voices in worship (24; 118; 132); for such psalms Gunkel used the term 'liturgies'.

It is often thought convenient (following Gunkel) to reckon with a class of *Royal Psalms*, which would have in common an obvious concern for the king. The psalms in question present the work of the king as chief servant of God's own reign from Zion. They may refer to ceremonies of inaugurating or renewing the human king's reign (2; 110), or ceremonies of his wedding (45); prayers or blessings may be spoken for him (20; 21; 72); he may pray for salvation (89; 101; 132; 144) or give thanks for it (18). But here again, the classification should be regarded as only a useful preliminary. The situations and aims reflected here are diverse and there are other psalms, perhaps many others, which will also have been psalms of the king, as indeed the traditional association with the founder of the dynasty, David, suggests.

The study of forms in the psalms reveals a wonderful

interplay of tradition and originality. Broad types of psalm came into being, each traditional for a particular situation. In flexible fashion the elements of psalmody – calls to praise, petitions and so on – could be drawn on in various ways to suit various purposes. Words and phrases in these elements were often from a traditional stock. And yet there is seldom an impression of staleness. The tradition, never rigid, seems to have provided a spring-board from which individual poetic gifts could leap. The study of similarities in form and phrasing is a necessary approach to this ancient poetry and contributes to the interpretation of words, sentences and whole poems. But in the end it does not reveal a tedious formalism in this Hebrew poetry, but shows an ever-rising spring of inspiration.

The poets
We have been concerned with poetry. But who were the poets? Our ancient sources show a gradual development towards the custom which existed around New Testament times of speaking of the Psalms as a whole as the work of David. The collection itself is simply entitled in the Hebrew *The Book of Praises* or just *Praises*. It has five main sections, each marked with a conclusion of praise (see the end of Pss.41; 72; 89; 106; 150). These divisions reflect the process of earlier collections being brought together; at the end of Psalm 72, for example, a note states that 'the prayers of David son of Jesse are ended'.

Most psalms have a heading of some kind, and here we often meet obscure technical terms for the type of psalm and the manner of performing it. We also meet personal names which could indicate supposed authorship or a collection under the name and guardianship of that person. The heading of Psalm 90 names Moses, while over 72 and 127 we find 'Solomon'. Some names indicate guilds of psalm-singers at the temple or their founding fathers ('the sons of Korah' Pss.42, 44–9, 84–5, 87–8; 'Asaph' 50, 73–83; 'Heman' 88; 'Ethan' 89). By far the most frequent is 'David', heading seventy-three psalms. Over thirteen of these there is also a note roughly indicating an episode in David's career as the supposed occasion of composition by him (3, 7, 18, 34, 51, 54, 56, 57, 59, 60, 63, 142). The details of the psalm-headings in the Greek translation, however, vary considerably from the Hebrew, and the likelihood is that the headings were developed and varied down the centuries. The ancient technical phrases will have been augmented here and there by notes of later scribes based on their own deductions or later usage.

Another ancient source reflecting views of the origin and use of the psalms is the Books of Chronicles (especially 1 Chr. 15–16; 25). Here we notice the setting of worship at the temple, the founding authority of David, and the guilds of singers at the temple. David is also said to have made instruments (2 Chr. 7.6, cf. Amos 6.5; Neh. 12.36). About 190 BC Jesus ben Sirach gathers all the tradition into his poetic tribute to David:

> In all he did he gave thanks,
>   giving glory to the Holy One, the Most High.
> He sang praise with all his heart,
>   expressing his love for his maker.
> He appointed singers to stand before the altar
>   and sing sweet music to the lyre.
> He gave beauty to the festivals
>   and fixed their times through all the year,
> when they should praise the Lord's name,
>   the sanctuary resounding from early morning.
>   (Ecclus. 47.8–10)

In assessing this tradition about the origin of the Psalms, one can recognize firstly that David's personal gifts as composer, singer and player are well attested. In addition to the story of his service as lyre-player to Saul (1 Sam.16.14ff.), there are plausible examples of his art in the histories:

> How are the mighty fallen
>   in the midst of the battle!
>   (2 Sam.1.17f.)

The death of a fool
  should Abner die?
Unbound were your hands and your feet,
  with fetters not hurt.
A falling before the sons of iniquity
  you fell.

                                      (2 Sam.3.33–4)

An ancient poem about royal duty is recorded as his last
words:

The oracle of the man the High One raised,
  the anointed of the God of Jacob,
  sweetest singer of Israel.

                                      (2 Sam.23.1f.)

In the modern study of the Psalms there are indications that
support the basic importance of David. The most fruitful
period of psalmody is now often recognized to be that of the
Davidic monarchy, and especially in the time of its early
strength. While the temple of Solomon would seem likely to
open a new era for worship and its music, there was some form
of important sanctuary at Jerusalem in David's time, attested
for example in 2 Samuel 12.20: 'David rose from the ground
and washed and anointed himself and changed his mantle and
went into the house of the Lord and prostrated himself.'
Certainly David was responsible for making Jerusalem the
centre of Israel's worship and for founding the dynasty which
presided over worship there for over four centuries. Central
themes of the Psalms thus clearly spring from his work, and
though the guilds of psalm-singers will often have been the
authors as well as the performers, there was good reason to
look back to David as the founder and director of the whole
tradition of musical worship in Jerusalem.
  It is interesting that some modern scholars have thought
that the worshipper in many of the Psalms uttered by an
individual is a king, and that in addition to the Psalms sung by
or for a king at the grand ceremonies there are many arising

from particular royal crises – sickness, invasion, conspiracies and so on. In some of these cases it could be that the king was David himself.

All in all, one may say that the Psalms are a collection spanning centuries of composition and using forms and expressions rooted in much more ancient times and in a wide area of the Near East. Hereditary guilds of psalmists generally composed, performed and preserved them under the direction of the Davidic kings and the authorities who succeeded them. David, who first made Jerusalem the centre of Israel's worship and the home of the ark of the covenant, was certainly the immediate founder of the tradition. That he himself composed and performed psalms is likely, though it is hardly possible to say which. That he had the musical gifts and the creative and passionate heart is well attested. It is plausible that in some psalms it is David who pours out his grief before the Lord, and in some psalms, too, it is David who gives thanks to the holy one and sings praise with all his heart.

3

ARCHITECTURE AND
THE PSALMS

For all its innovations, modern architecture still has much in common with its forerunner in the period of the Psalms. Then as now the construction had to be blended with the character of the site; then as now the buildings had to serve their purpose efficiently; then as now the good architect expressed truth, embodied ideas, evoked joy and uplifted the spirit.

The beloved city: site and development
For poems of such spiritual and universal power, the Psalms are concerned to a surprising degree with one little town and its buildings. The thoughts of the exiles express this concern most poignantly:

> By the rivers of Babylon,
> there we sat down and wept
> as we remembered Zion.

(137.1)

The passionate little psalm uses twice the name 'Zion' and three times 'Jerusalem'; both names denote the sacred city, though 'Zion' is the name especially favoured in the poetic traditions which dwell on the city's significance. All the skill of this lyrist's cunning hand, all the agility of his singing tongue have been dedicated to the Lord who has revealed himself in Jerusalem. Therefore that place, with its hills and valleys and ascents and walls, its houses and its sanctuary, still claims first love:

How should we sing the songs of the Lord
on alien soil?
When my memory of you, Jerusalem, fades,
then wither my right hand!
Let my tongue stick to my palate,
when I remember you no more,
when I no longer set Jerusalem
above my highest joy!

(137.4–6)

The blending of construction and natural site is reflected in several psalms. But first we note some facts of the location. There were certain practical requirements which had governed its choice: its walls had to rise above steep ascents for purposes of defence, yet it must not be too hard of access for peacetime life, and above all it should have a dependable supply of water. A royal city should also be sited to control routes and provinces. Now Jerusalem lay beside the route from north to south down the watershed of the mountains, and near ways to west and east. Lying between the ancient territories of the rival northerly and southerly tribal blocks, its very location could evoke hopes of reconciliation and unity. Of the two parallel ridges which it covered in later times, that on the east is the lower and narrower, and yet its southern and lower end carried the original city, which was already a thousand years old when captured by David c.1000 BC (Fig. 3). Here the city stood on a narrow spur below the continuation of the ridge northwards, lower also than the hills around, and quite overlooked by the Mount of Olives on the east. Yet this spur rose abruptly from the valleys. What was more, it was blessed with a spring, Gihon, low on its eastern slope.

The architects worked sensitively with these natural conditions. This was a well-established tradition, for siting and fortification were matters of life and death, and David and his line inherited in the old city solid work from bronze age times. The numerous excavations of ancient Palestinian towns in recent years show how methods of construction, fortification,

44

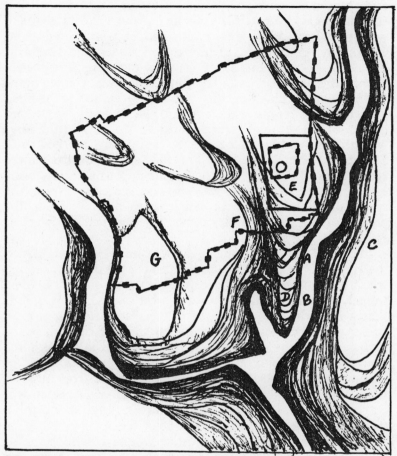

Fig. 3 Site of Jerusalem with present Old City walls

Key:
- A. Spring
- B. Kidron Valley
- C. Mount of Olives
- D. David's city
- E. Solomon's extensions
- F. Expansion in later monarchy
- G. Hellenistic expansion

and securement of water were varied and improved to meet the challenges of a particular site and of the developing arts of warfare. The capacity of the spur had been increased about 1800 BC by the building of terraces on stone-filled platforms down the steep eastern slope, pushing out some fifty metres beyond the summit area and two-thirds of the way down to the Kidron Valley. This structure was reinforced and maintained until the destruction of the city and the Exile in 586 BC, and could be the feature of Jerusalem called 'the Millo' ('the Fill') which David and his successors are said to have worked on (2 Sam. 5.9; 1 Kings 9.15, etc). This bold extension also had the advantage of bringing the east wall as near as possible to the spring. A gate in the east wall gave convenient access to the spring and the walled pool which surrounded it. From the pool a conduit carried water to another pool and gardens just south of the city.

In time of war, the spring could now more easily be guarded to deny water to the enemy and to protect the tunnels through which some of the water was diverted into the city. The oldest tunnel, large and arched, led water westwards down to a deep shaft within the city. At the top of the shaft a sloping passage rose to steps which in turn ascended to the surface. This seems to have been the route through which David's task-force stormed to capture the city from the Jebusites. Quite a maze of tunnels developed as adjustments were made from time to time, and eventually the remarkable tunnel of Hezekiah was cut, winding deep into the rocky hill to lead the water into a reservoir on the south-western slope of the spur.

The defensive value of the hillsides will have been increased by the construction of some form of glacis. Although this can hardly be traced today, there is much evidence from other Palestinian sites that before and during the royal period main walls were protected and enhanced by an outer ring (Hebrew *hel*). This might consist of beaten earth, stones and plaster, forming a steep, solid and slippery band sloping away beneath the main walls. The walls themselves were commonly built to great widths and reinforced by bastions and towers combined with angles, salients and recesses. The long wall on the west

46

followed the crest of the narrow spur, so that the old city covered scarcely eleven acres.

Solomon the builder

It seems that it was within this confined city that David first established the sanctuary of the Lord, placing the ark in a tent shrine, with space about it for sacrifice and assembly (2 Sam. 6). Outside the city, on the higher part of the ridge to the north, he is said to have built an altar and offered sacrifice (2 Sam. 24.25) and at least planned a temple (2 Chr. 3.1). At all events, Solomon carried through a great development there about 965 BC, building a complex of royal and sacred buildings, including 'the house of the Lord' (1 Kings 5f.). The most arresting feature of Jerusalem today, the vast platform of the temple area, dates from Herod's reconstruction begun in 20 BC, extending the plateau of the hill with vaulted substructures and walls of massive stone blocks. This great work, however, was not entirely new. It is clear that its eastern line incorporates that of its predecessor. Herod has added to the length of the platform on north and south and has boldly extended the western boundary, the present 'Wailing Wall', over the central valley. But Solomon's platform was extensive too, providing for a fine and spacious sanctuary area.

There can be no question of the skill of Solomon's architects. Obtained by treaty from Phoenicia, they were builders and craftsmen of the highest order. A small sample of their masonry has been found at Jerusalem similar to the splendid Phoenician work known at Samaria, Byblos and Tyre. We can therefore form a good impression of the Solomonic constructions on the northern part of the ridge. The finer buildings will have been beautifully faced with large ashlar stone blocks, cut to perfect smoothness and a precise fitting. For the heavy walls, foundation courses and platforms, the great stones would have dressed margins around irregular bosses. Pilaster columns were ornamented with capitals of the proto-Ionic type (Fig. 4).

Much of the rest of the city will have remained in the traditional local style with undressed chunks of stone packed

Fig. 4 Pilaster capital from Jerusalem

together rather as in a Cumberland sheep-wall; such construction was often finished with mud plaster and developed to a
great thickness for the outer defences. The city walls were now
extended to link up with the new developments. In the course
of time the defences also embraced settlements on the parallel
western ridge, though the areas and dates have been much
disputed. A surviving section of wall, west of the south-west
corner of Herod's platform and part way up the western hill,
has been thought to be the wall built by Hezekiah a little
before 700 BC (2 Chr. 32.5). Perhaps it enclosed the quarters
called 'the Mishneh' ('the Second District', 2 Kings 22.14 and
Zeph. 1.10) and 'the Maktesh' ('the Basin', Zeph. 1.11), a
scene of noisy trading, perhaps a hollow in the valley west of
the temple area. For the earlier part of the royal period, so
important for the core of the Psalms, we should probably
continue to think only of a heavily fortified and compact city
on the eastern ridge, and it is agreed that in the main post-
exilic period, the sixth to the third centuries BC, the city there
was even more contracted, the ancient terraced extension
being collapsed and abandoned. The Maccabean age saw
renewed fortification on the western ridge, and this area was
utilized further in Herod's Jerusalem, with two splendid
viaducts spanning the valley between the two ridges.

The city's aspect

A famous story relates how David rose from his siesta and took the air in the late afternoon by walking on the palace roof, which afforded views into the court-yards of nearby houses (2 Sam. 11). The tradition of flat-roofed buildings in Palestine continued into our own times. Sometimes you may see rollers kept on the roof ready to roll out the mud-plaster after rain. In this mud wild grass or grain will take root, but so shallowly that of all Palestine's verdure it is the quickest to perish under the hot sun and desert winds. The singer of Psalm 129 also knew a Zion of flat-roofed, mud-sealed buildings:

> Stricken with shame and turning their backs
> be all the haters of Zion!
> Let them be like grass on the roofs
> withering before it can grow up,
> leaving no handful for the reaper,
> no sheaf for the harvester's bosom!
>
> (129.5–7)

We picture ancient Jerusalem, then, for most of its centuries, as of compact character, with its flat-roofed buildings rising for the most part in close array on the crests and upper slopes of the hills, rather as Lachish, a city some twenty-five miles to the south-west, has been portrayed from Assyrian sculptures and excavations (*Oxford Bible Atlas*, 1974, 104–5). Rare and of great utility were the spaces, notably those within and adjoining the elaborate gateways and those of the courts of the temple and palaces. Like a well-defined castle, Jerusalem was a city that could be gone around and surveyed admiringly, though Psalm 48 teaches the congregation that their tour should speak to them of God, not men:

> Go round Zion and circle about her,
> count her towers, take note of her rampart,
> reckon up her bastions,
> that you may tell the next generation
> that he is God, our God for ever and ever!
>
> (48.12–14)

The siting of the temple high on the ridge gave it an appropriate majesty as it rose well above the old city:

> At your temple above Jerusalem
> kings in procession bear gifts to you ...
> above Israel is his majesty
> and his glory is in the clouds,
> from his sanctuary the awesome God appears.
>
> (68.29,34–5)

The elevation can become almost transfigured in the eyes of faith:

> City of our God,
> his holy mountain,
> beautiful in elevation,
> joy of all the world,
> mountain of Zion,
> peak of Zaphon!
>
> (48.1–2)

The architects would have no difficulty in making the immediate approaches to the temple impressive ascents, with steeply rising road and steps:

> God has ascended with acclamation,
> the Lord with the noise of the horn!
>
> (47.5)

> There the tribes ascend,
> the tribes of the Lord,
> as ordained for Israel,
> to give praise to the name of the Lord.
>
> (122.4)

This modest elevation, then, was yet enough to represent the idea of God's place above the world, though prophets might sing of a day when the ascendancy would be clear to all:

50

This shall happen at the end of the years:
the mountain of the house of the Lord
shall be made highest of the mountains
and raised above the hills,
and all nations shall stream to it
and many peoples shall go there, saying
'Come, let us go up to the mountain of the Lord,
to the house of the God of Jacob!'

(Isa. 2.2f.)

Meanwhile the higher mountains around Jerusalem could be seen as protection and as suggestive of the Lord's shield about his people:

See, Jerusalem surrounded by mountains –
so the Lord surrounds his people!

(Ps. 125.2)

From these higher hills, the approaching pilgrims would gain a view of the holy city lying compact within its walls and turrets, its stone clean and honey-coloured in the strong sun. Their thoughts were led to unity and brotherhood in the place of worship:

O Jerusalem, built as a city
that is compacted together!

(122.3f.)

See, how good and sweet it is
when brothers dwell together as one!

(133.1f.)

In the love which brings together and binds the worshippers of God is the blessing of true life. Like the holy oil poured over the high priest's head at his consecration, or like the dew running down from Mount Hermon, so the life-giving grace runs down through the fellowship of Jerusalem:

51

For there by the Lord's command
runs the blessing,
life for evermore!

(133.3)

Symbols of life
This theme of the holy city as the centre of life was of basic
importance. The Lord was mysteriously there, and from his
house in Zion life flowed into the world:

How precious is your fidelity, Lord!
Mankind shelters in the shade of your wings.
They feast on the fat of your house
and you give them drink from your delicious streams.
Beside you rises the spring of life
and in your light we see light.

(36.7f.)

A city on the Judean mountains might not seem an easy place
for the architects to symbolize life and fertility; but the harsh
desert falling away to the east, the annual drought of six
months or more, the absence of perennial rivers and the
scarcity of springs, made every sign of vitality more striking
than in lands of perpetual greenness and moisture. The
ornamentation of panelling and stonework in the temple was
in the form of trees, flowers and fruit, especially palms,
gourds, lotus and pomegranate. Great basins of water in the
temple court reminded worshippers of the Lord's mastery of
the oceans and rivers, whereby he sent the rains at his
command. We read, for example, of a massive bronze bowl
called 'the Sea', supported by twelve bronze oxen (1 Kings
7.23f.) The golden lampstands before the inner sanctuary
were also signs of life. Above all, well-tended trees in the
temple courts and beside the processional way were important
for a building serving the theme of life. A psalm thus speaks of
the man pompous in his own wealth as soon to be like an
uprooted plant, while the man who puts all his trust in God's
grace is like a tree in the temple courts:

52

But I am like a green olive-tree in the house of God,
I trust in God's fidelity for ever and ever.

(52.8)

Or again, the wicked rise up everywhere like the grass in
spring, which, however, soon withers in the summer drought
and heat, while

the righteous man sprouts like a palm-tree,
like a cedar in the Lebanon he spreads.
Those planted in the house of the Lord
sprout up in the courts of our God,
in old age still bearing fruit,
continuing moist and green.

(92.12–14)

Not far from the base of the temple hill, the spring Gihon
filled its surrounding pool and sent currents under the city and
beside it to the gardens and orchards, while in the rainy season
the Kidron valley, under the east wall, itself ran with water
and its banks awoke to vivid green. What this water might
become in the mind of the worshipper is shown by the vision
Ezekiel, who saw a renewed temple from under which flowed
forth a stream, life from the throne of God:

Here water was running out eastwards from under the
terrace of the house (of the Lord) – for the house faced
east – and this water was running down from under the
south corner of the house to the south of the altar. And he
led me out by the north gate and brought me round the
outer road to the outer gate facing east, and here was
water rippling down from the south corner ...
and wherever the stream runs, everything awakes to
life.

(Ezek. 47.1f.)

Thus, for all the limitations of the site, the meaning was
conveyed that in this place the worshipper was quickened with

life. Here he was with the Lord who provided green pasture and refreshing water, whose table was spread and who gave a brimming cup (Ps. 23).

The stronghold
More readily the city spoke to the pilgrims of the stronghold which God provides. Its character as virtually a castle above steep slopes suited the faith in a God who offered to his worshippers at Zion refuge, shelter, stability. Today the summit of the living rock of the temple hill forms the holiest place, beautifully housed by the Muslim 'Dome of the Rock'. We cannot be certain of the function of this summit in Solomon's temple, and in particular whether it rose within the inmost shrine, the Holy of Holies, or whether it underlay the great altar in the court. But 'Rock' was a favourite designation of God, and his protection is often described with images from mountainous strongholds. The sanctuary-city rose up in such solid strength that it seemed not unworthy of its significance as God's seat, and indeed of his constructing:

> Then he chose the tribe of Judah
> and Mount Zion which he loved,
> and he built his sanctuary like the heavenly heights,
> like the earth which he has founded for ever.
>
> (78.68–9)

But the stress always falls on God, not the city, as the fortress and shelter:

> God shows himself in her bastions
> to be a high tower of defence.
>
> (48.3)

> The Lord of hosts is with us,
> the God of Jacob is a high tower for us.
>
> (46.7)

You will lead me on to a rock far above me,
for you will become a refuge for me,
a strong bastion against the enemy.

(61.2–3)

The Lord is a crag for me,
my fortress and my deliverer,
my God, my rock on which I find safety.

(18.2)

When at last, in 586 BC, the city was destroyed, it could be
known that the true fortress, God himself, remained, and
when he willed he could command the resurrection of these
dear stones:

But you, Lord, keep your throne for ever
and your name will be invoked through all generations.
Come, Lord, show pity for Zion!
Surely the time to deal kindly with her,
the time appointed, surely it has come!
For we, your servants, love her very stones
and feel pity for her dust.

(102.12–14)

On the holy way
These have been overall impressions of the situation and
construction of Jerusalem and their reflection in the Psalms.
Guided by further psalm references, we now make the journey
in orderly progress from outside the city into the inmost
shrine, pondering the meaning which the ancient worshippers
found in this place.

We begin outside on the sacred road, which probably led in
from the wilderness on the east. The ceremonies at the
festivals included important processions between the temple
and stations beyond the city. Enactment was thereby made of
God's going forth against the forces of evil and his return in
triumph. The route along which his march was symbolized,
probably by conveyance of the ark, was thus a holy way. The

55

throngs who attended his procession experienced his revelation and salvation and united with the ministers in responses of homage and praise. The pilgrim would especially remember these great scenes on the sacred way outside the city, and at the outset of a new pilgrimage he would look forward to them. On such a a person Psalm 84 declares a blessing:

> Happy are the people who draw strength from you,
> the procession-ways being in their hearts!
>
> (84.5)

The word used here, *mesilla*, denotes a road built up with banks, cleared, and in special cases paved with stones. The calls to repair these processional routes by clearing of stones, filling of holes and banking up edges entered into the language of religion. By such phrases prophets would announce the approach of the Lord:

> Bank up, bank up the raised way,
> clear it of stones ...
> See your salvation comes,
> see, his reward is with him!
>
> (Isa. 62.10f)

> A raised way shall be there
> and it shall be called the holy way.
> There the redeemed shall walk.
>
> (Isa. 35.8f.)

> In the wilderness clear the way of the Lord,
> in the desert set in order the raised way for our God!
> (Isa. 40.3)

> Bank up (the road) for the Rider of the clouds!
> (Ps. 68.4)

What scenes there were on the sacred road! –

56

They see your procession, O God,
the procession of my God, my king, into the sanctuary!

(68.24)

There the Lord revealed his glory, and all together beheld it in awe and were replenished (Isa. 40.5).

Through the rampart and walls
The raised way would finally ascend the steep hillside and pass through the outer rampart, which was some kind of glacis or forewall combining with the slope to keep attackers from the walls. Psalm 122 links this all-embracing fortification, as also the towers at the gates and angles of the walls, with the very name 'Jerusalem', which meant 'foundation of peace':

Peace be within your rampart,
prosperity within your bastions!

(122.7)

Worshippers might be summoned to go round the circumference of the city and meditate on this rampart and the bastions rising above the walls:

Take note of her rampart,
reckon up her bastions!

(48.12–13)

Their sturdy appearance around the holy city made them suitable signs of the abiding protection of God.

Above the rampart rose the walls which embraced both temple courts and city. Parts would be in the casemate style, where thick inner and outer sides enclose a cavity sufficient to make guard-rooms and galleries for the defenders. Other sections were solid, but still of great width: one surviving section is five metres wide. Such stout walls gave ample room for processions to move along the top. Even the wall of Nehemiah, hastily built of rough stones and 2.75 metres thick in one surviving section, carried notable processions. At the dedication service shortly after 445 BC two parties of dignitaries and musicians mounted the wall on the west and moved along in opposite directions, to join up again on the eastern side and descend into the temple court (Neh. 12.31f.). Thus the enemy's jibe that this new wall would not withstand the weight of a fox (Neh. 4.3) was fortunately disproved! A psalm tells of a grimmer occasion. Instead of the angels of peace and truth which should ever patrol upon the walls and through the streets, the psalmist sees spectres of anarchy trooping the rounds:

> I see Violence and Strife in the city,
> day and night they circle her upon her walls,
> and Mischief and Trouble are within her, Ruin also,
> while Oppression and Fraud haunt her square.
>
> (55.10–11)

Such thick walls were eloquent of the hand of God. Truly, he must be the builder and maintainer if they were to stand:

> Do good to Zion in your favour!
> You will build up the walls of Jerusalem.
>
> (51.18)

> Unless the Lord builds the house,
> vainly its builders toil on it.
> Unless the Lord keeps the city,
> vainly the watchmen wake.
>
> (127.1)

In the gates
In the walls the gateways were set with cunning, so that those approaching were exposed to the attention of the defenders. Watched from a tower, those entering might have to pass through a passage between two or three pairs of gates and perhaps have to turn at right angles. Between the inner and outer surfaces of the walls, there was room within the gateway for guard-houses and for various public transactions, which

58

might spill over into the space of the approaches. Here disputes were adjudicated, and the man with many sons would not be intimidated when he contested his case there with his adversaries:

> Sons come by the Lord's gift,
> he rewards with fruit of the womb.
> Like arrows in the hand of a marksman,
> so are the sons of our youth.
> Happy are those who have filled their quiver with them!
> They will not be put to shame
> when they argue with their enemies in the gate.
>
> (127.3–5)

Here also a holy man might preach (Jer. 7), or a person might testify of God's help:

> Be merciful to me, Lord,
> see what I suffer from those who hate me,
> O God who shall raise me from the gates of death,
> that I may recount all your praises
> in the gates of dear Zion
> and celebrate your salvation!
>
> (9.13–14)

Here Zion's gates are the gates of life in contrast to the gloomy portals of the underworld.

At the gates a festal procession might pause for liturgical responses. One wonders what structure of gate may be implied by the call 'Lift up your heads, O gates!' Perhaps the psalmist feels an anomaly that the symbols of God's presence should have to go under any framework. This passage from Psalm 24 does illustrate how a deeper meaning was seen within the forms of architecture and ceremony. The march up the sacred way, the approach to the temple gate, all signified the triumph of the Creator, who brought order out of chaos and in his glory and supremacy preserved life and goodness. So the road was the road of heaven and the gates the eternal gates of the heavenly city, and the worshippers were in the presence of the universal Lord:

> Lift up your heads, you gates,
> be lifted up, eternal doors,
> that the King of glory may come in!

(24.7f.)

These gates were spoken of as *his* gates, giving entrance to *his* house. One should enter with songs of praise that recognized his greatness, and with humble regard for righteousness of life:

> Come before him with singing ...
> enter his gates with thanksgiving,
> his courts with praise!

(100.2–4)

Psalm 118 may be understood to accompany the entry of the Davidic king in a ceremony of deep significance. Outside the city, on this view, he endured rites of affliction, in sign of the tribulations in face of which men come to believe in the Lord as their saviour:

> Sorely the Lord chastised me,
> but to death he did not give me.

(118.18)

His entry through the 'gate of the Lord' is now a sign of his 'righteousness', that is, his new trust in the Lord, overflowing in his testimony:

> Open for me the gates of righteousness!
> I will enter them and give thanks to the Lord.
> This is the gate of the Lord.
> The righteous shall enter it.

(118.19–20)

Over the courts

Through the Lord's gates one reached his courts (100.4), which are sometimes included in the expression 'the house of the Lord'. There was an 'inner court' (1 Kings 6.36) specifically for the temple area, an outer or 'great court' (1 Kings 7.12) which embraced also the adjoining palaces and halls. Further subdivisions appear from time to time, such as the 'new court' (2 Chr. 20.5) and an 'upper court' (Jer. 36.10). Much of the work of the sanctuary took place in these open, partly paved areas, especially the sacrifices on the great altar and prayers and praises of the massed assembly. As on the site today, the proportion of the small sacred buildings to the wide courts under the open sky gave beauty and peace. Here the worshippers felt themselves to be in the Lord's house, and they ate and drank in fellowship with him from the sacrifices which fulfilled the vows made in time of trouble:

> Ascribe to the Lord the glory of his name!
> Carry tribute and enter into his courts!
>
> (Ps. 96.8)

> Happy the person you choose
> and bring near to dwell in your courts!
> We shall be satisfied with the rich fare of your house,
> the holy place of your temple.
>
> (65.4)

In the surrounding battlements and turrets birds would nest, and may have been left unmolested in the spirit of the prophet's words:

> They shall not harm,
> they shall not destroy
> on all my holy mountain.
>
> (Isa. 11.9)

The eagerness of the little creatures for their nests gives an image of the worshipper's longing to rest with God, whose

61

presence is known in the courts and by the altar. Love wells up for the place and its buildings because he is there, ready to recreate his people in joyful life:

> How lovely your abode, Lord of hosts!
> My soul pined and fainted for the courts of the Lord.
> My heart, my whole body cried out for the living God.
> Now my soul is a bird that has found its home,
> a swallow building a nest to lay her young
> close to your altars, Lord of hosts,
> my King and my God.
>
> (84.1–3)

A scene of thanksgiving in the courts is portrayed by Psalm 116, perhaps a king's testimony. The story of rescue from anguish to joy is told as the vows are fulfilled 'in the presence of all his people'. The grateful man stands before the altar and raises high the cup which celebrates his salvation. It probably contains a drink-offering to be poured out to the Lord. In this sacred spot he is in the heart of the city of the Lord, a unity embracing the temple, and so his last words affectionately turn his address to the city itself:

> What can I return to the Lord
> for all he has done for me?
> I will raise the cup of salvation
> and proclaim the name of the Lord.
> I will fulfil my vows to the Lord
> before all his assembled people . . .
> in the courts of the house of the Lord,
> in the midst of you, Jerusalem!
>
> (116.12f.)

By the altar and mounted basins
The great altar stood in the court, well to the east of the temple, and in the space between temple and altar a choir of priests would lead supplications in time of need:

Between the temple-porch and the altar
let the priests weep,
those who served the Lord,
and let them say,
'Lord, have pity on your people!'

(Joel 2.17)

Priestly singers, 'servants of the Lord', would also stand in the
courts to lead praises:

Praise the name of the Lord,
praise it, servants of the Lord,
as you stand in the house of the Lord,
in the courts of the house of our God!

(Ps. 135.1–2)

At night also, when torches would be lit, the singers stood in
the open to raise their hands towards the shrine and bless the
Lord:

Come, bless the Lord,
all you servants of the Lord,
standing through the nights in the house of the Lord!
Lift your hands to the holy place
and bless the Lord!

(134.1–2)

So they could turn again to the people and pass on what they
had received from the Lord:

May the Lord, the maker of heaven and earth,
bless you also from Zion!

(134.3)

The situation of the altar in the spacious court made it well
suited to encircling movements. Ten bronze basins of water on
wheeled stands stood near in groups of five (1 Kings 7.27f.)
and perhaps are used in the rite of Psalm 26:

I will wash my palms in innocency
and circle your altar, Lord,
that I may announce with a song of thanksgiving,
may recount all your miracles.

(26.6–7)

In Psalm 118 the procession has passed along the sacred way
from outside the city and has ascended through the 'gate of the
Lord' into the courts and towards the great bronze altar. From
each corner of the altar rose a kind of spike, the 'horns',
thought of as points of holy power. To these horns the
companies of worshippers were now linked, either by cords or
(on another translation) by green branches as they approached, and perhaps encircled, the altar with dancing step:

Bind the dance with cords
up to the horns of the altar!

(118.27)

To serve at the bronze altar, the minister had to ascend
upon it, as did King Ahaz (2 Kings 16.12), and it is likely that
the shape of the altar in Ezekiel's vision (Ezek. 43.13–17),
with steps leading to the summit, was that of the actual altar.
Steps could be symbolic of the heavenly ascent, and probably
had a similar significance before the inner shrine, before the
temple-porch, in the temple gateway, and before the king's
throne. It is possible that the 'stairs' or 'ascents' mentioned in
the titles of Psalms 120–134 have some connection with
singing on such flights of steps in the approach to the temple.

The house at the centre of the world
Beyond the altar one approached the temple proper, its
entrance facing east. Outside the entrance were two free-
standing bronze pillars crowned with bronze capitals of lotus
form and decorated each with two hundred pomegranates (1
Kings 7.15f.). Each pillar had a name, which some have
thought to be abbreviated forms of prayers or oracles supporting the dynasty of David and reflected also in the Psalms.

Thus the name 'Boaz' resembles the beginning of Psalm 21: *'In your power* may the king rejoice, Lord!' But whatever the precise interpretation, these tall, gleaming pillars were eloquent of the order, stability and life which came only from the reign of God:

> When the earth reels and all that dwell on it,
> I alone set right its pillars.

(75.3)

> The Lord is King!
> Earth's ground is fixed
> and will not shake.

(93.1)

The temple building was an oblong which measured only about eighty-eight feet long, thirty feet wide and forty-four feet high. It was built of carefully cut stones in the Phoenician style with a layer of timber, it seems, between every three courses to give elasticity. (Another view is that there were three courses of stone, one of timber, and then a superstructure of brick.) The inside surface was entirely panelled with cedar and gold and the floor was covered with fir boards. The windows were in the upper part of the walls as in a clerestory. Whether the description in 1 Kings 6.4 refers to lattice work or to embrasures (sloping to a small outer aperture), the architect's intention will have been to moderate the entry of bright light, heat or rain. One entered first a porch or vestibule (the *Ulam*) and then the main room or nave (the *Heykal*). In the nave stood a gold altar for incense, ten lampstands and a gold table bearing twelve loaves. Finally one came to the inner shrine (the *Debir*) which was probably reached up a flight of steps and through a curtain of gold chains (1 Kings 6.21). Here in darkness were the ark and two winged cherubs of wood and gold. The cherubs, a kind of angel, may well have resembled the figures carved in Phoenician style on ivory plaques and having a body of a winged lion and a human face (Fig. 5).

The particulars of the 'house of the Lord' rarely appear in

Fig. 5 Ivory cherub-figure from Samaria

the Psalms, which however testify to a great wealth of religious experience mediated by this place of modest proportions and simple equipment. The inmost shrine, the *Debir*, is named only in Psalm 28, where it is very likely the king who prays from the court, directing voice and hands to the temple:

> Hear the noise of my supplications
> as I cry to you,
> as I lift my hands
> to your holy shrine (*Debir*)! (28.2)

Where the word *Heykal* does occur, it may be intended in its wider meaning, 'Palace (of God), temple' (5.7; 68.29; 79.1; 138.2). The restricted meaning 'nave' may perhaps be found in Psalm 48; a symbolic action, showing God's protection of Jerusalem, has been performed:

> We have represented your fidelity, O God,
> in the midst of your sacred hall (*Heykal*)!
>
> (48.9)

Even the ark, a portable chest containing the deeds of the covenant, is named only in Psalm 132, a passage which clearly shows how the divine presence is with the ark both in its processions and in its standing in the shrine:

> Arise, Lord, for (the procession to) your resting place,
> you and the ark of your power!
>
> (132.8)

'Power' here (*oz*) is a similar term to 'glory' (*kabod*) and both words can refer to the presence and revelation of God in his holy place and rites. It is likely that the presence of God in Psalm 24, which five times cites God's title 'King of glory', was enacted with the ark. Likewise we should imagine the ark as used in the procession of Psalm 68, for it again calls on the Lord to 'arise' as in the old ceremony of lifting the ark (Num. 10.35):

> Let God arise,
> let his enemies be scattered!
>
> (68.1)

As enthroned King of the world, God is imagined to have a footstool, which can be the ark (1 Chr. 28.2; Ps. 132.7), or the temple (Isa. 60.13), or Jerusalem (Lam. 2.1), or indeed the earth (Isa. 66.1). This variation is interesting, suggesting how the smallness of cultic objects did not hinder the great range of their symbolism. Thus the dark inmost shrine, a cube of scarcely thirty feet, was symbolically the throne-room of God, the two cherubs representing or upholding his throne:

> You who are enthroned over the cherubim,
> shine out . . .
> greet us with radiant face
> that we may be saved!
>
> (80.1–3)

> The Lord is King . . .
> he is enthroned over the cherubim,
> the Lord appears mightily in Zion
> and high is he above all the peoples!
>
> (99.1–2)

A bridge to heaven

From such texts, and many more, it can be seen how the little building and its sparse equipment are transfigured in religious faith and imagination. From poets and prophets the people catch the vision of Zion as the place of meeting with the Lord, the almighty Creator:

> God of gods, the Lord speaks
> and summons the world
> from the rising of the sun to its setting.
> From Zion, perfection of beauty,
> God gives his radiance.
>
> (50.1–2)

Their soul pined and fainted for the courts of the Lord because 'the God of gods will be seen in Zion' (84.2,5). The architecture of this holy city, with its sacred ways, ramparts, walls, turrets, gates, courts, temple, halls and houses, achieved its deepest purpose in serving the religion where such experience of contact with God arose. In this holy site the worshipper believed himself to be before God's 'face', felt the power of God's 'name' (in which was his very person), was sheltered under his 'wings', was replenished by his 'light', and

beheld his 'beauty'. All that served this experience was
precious – the stones, the fellowship, the rites; but the essence
was the meeting with God. This was the 'one thing' most
earnestly to desire:

> One thing I ask of the Lord
> and that I will seek for:
> that I may dwell in the house of the Lord
> all the days of my life,
> to behold the beauty of the Lord
> and seek guidance in his temple ...
> Your face, Lord, I will seek.

> (27.4–8)

> So in the sanctuary I would behold you,
> seeing your power and your glory.

> (63.2)

The strongest expressions of this kind may originate in prayers
of kings, for it was their calling, as 'the Lord's anointed', to be
especially close in that presence. With prayerful preparation
the supplicant would sleep in the temple in quest of such
revelation:

> But I in your favour shall behold your face,
> on awakening I shall be satisfied with your form.

> (17.15)

The construction and usages of the sanctuary, then, had a
bold aim: to bring before the worshippers the realities of
heaven. That God was transcendent, abiding far above his
world in supreme majesty, was not in question, as the Psalms
show again and again with imagination of his palace-temple
high above the heavens. But to these transcendent realities
men were brought near through the ministry of the temple,
and so might experience the Creator's very 'face' and 'form'.
So all the parts of the sanctuary that we have been considering
were 'holy', God's holy things and places, just as the heavenly

residence itself was holy. The term denotes what is especially close to God, imbued with his person, and not to be encroached upon by presumptuous or heedless men. As 'holy', the roadway, the mountain, the courts, the temple, are not just things of this world, but give contact with the heavenly and divine. By them one came in awe-inspiring directness before God.

In illustration of this crucial point we note Psalm 2, which speaks of Zion as God's 'holy mountain', that is, the place of his presence where at his right hand sits the Davidic king; but the psalm also pictures how God is laughing at his foes from his throne in heaven. Or again, Psalm 20 pictures God reaching out to help the king from the holy place at Zion (20.2), and also from his holy heaven (20.6). In Psalm 11 the singer has in mind the experience of nearness afforded by the temple when he speaks of 'taking refuge in the Lord' and 'beholding his face', but he also thinks of God's 'holy temple' in its heavenly reality in order to stress how God's gaze can look down searchingly upon all human deeds:

> But the Lord is in his holy temple.
> Over the heavens is the throne of the Lord
> and his eyes scan, his eyelids test the sons of men.
>
> (11.4)

Again, in Psalm 29 the worshippers in the temple who ascribe 'glory' to the Lord (29.9) are in union with the celestial beings who likewise bow and acknowledge his glory (29.1–2), and indeed they are in the presence of the Lord who is enthroned over heaven and earth (29.10). The priests in the temple are the serving-men in the residence of the Lord, and yet Psalm 113 calls upon these servants to praise him as high above all nations, manifest above the heavens.

The story of King Hezekiah comes to mind. To the house of the Lord he took the offensive letter and spread it out for the Lord to read. So concrete, so localized! But his prayer then addressed this God seated over the cherubs as sole Lord of all nations, sole Creator of heaven and earth (2 Kings 19.14f.).

The tiny Psalm 150 speaks volumes on this subject. At the house of the Lord musicians play before him, striving to please his ears and eyes with song and instruments and dances; but because that little place by symbol leads over the threshold of his heavenly palace, there the Lord is praised as in his most holy abode, the Lord enthroned over the sky vault which blazes with his glory; and there in little Zion is gathered up the praise of every breathing thing.

The architects of old Jerusalem, working for their livelihood with earth, water, trees, stone, bronze and gold, providing for defence, sustenance, trades and crafts, family life, administration and justice, teaching and worship, were found to have furthered a vision. They had made a city which came to be called 'city of God', place of 'the house of the Lord', where he would show himself in his beauty. To such a city the lyrist-singer gives all his passion and would be struck silent

> when I no longer set Jerusalem
> above my highest joy.

(137.6)

4

MUSIC AND THE PSALMS

Music and psalms always belonged together. The poetic words were intended to be sung and generally to be accompanied by instrumental music.

Occasionally there are headings over particular psalms which note what instruments should accompany them; Psalms 4 and 6 are to be sung with stringed instruments, Psalm 5 (though the translation is not certain) with pipes. More significantly, fifty-seven psalms happen to have in their headings the word rendered 'psalm' (Hebrew *mizmor*, Greek *psalmos*), a word which denotes a sacred chant accompanied by music. From the same root (*zamar*) come other words for the music of voice or instruments which the Psalms call for in praise of God. The verb resounds five times in an exciting passage where Coverdale renders it 'sing praises':

> God is gone up with a merry noise
> and the Lord with the sound of the trump.
> O sing praises (*zammeru*), sing praises unto our God,
> O sing praises, sing praises unto our King,
> for God is the King of all the earth.
> Sing ye praises with understanding.

(47.5–7)

The voices and instruments used in such music ring in our ears as the same beloved translator gives us:

Sing ye merrily unto God our strength,
make a cheerful noise unto the God of Jacob.
Take the psalm, bring hither the tabret,
the merry harp with the lute.
Blow up the trumpet in the new moon . . .
even in the time appointed,
and upon our solemn feast-day.

(81.1–3)

And Coverdale sees the orchestra of Psalm 150 as follows:

Praise him in the sound of the trumpet,
praise him upon the lute and harp,
praise him in the cymbals and dances,
praise him upon the strings and pipe,
praise him upon the well-tuned cymbals,
praise him upon the loud cymbals.

The leading role of music in worship is amply confirmed by accounts in the historical books. While the books of Chronicles, Ezra and Nehemiah dwell most on the subject, we find plenty of music in older sources, as in the story of David's festival:

And David and all the house of Israel were making merry before the Lord with all their might, with songs and lyres and harps and tambourines and castanets and cymbals.

(RSV of 2 Sam. 6.5)

The stringed instruments

Let us survey the particular instruments. For most we have to infer the details rather indirectly, helped especially by numerous portrayals of musicians in the art of Egypt and Mesopotamia. Systematic study by musicologists in recent decades has illumined ancient Near Eastern music and changed our understanding of many points.

Pride of place must be given to the *kinnor*, a kind of lyre. It is not clear that the three lyrists on a relief from Sennacherib's palace, filing before their guard, are Jewish captives as sometimes stated, and the lyres on Jewish coins from the revolt of AD 132–3 show later Greek influence. But the basic pattern is well-known: the lyre is a wooden instrument with a sound-box as a base, from which side-arms rise to join a cross-bar at the top. The strings, which could number between four and eleven, run from this bar down to the sound-box, where they might pass over a bridge. The Jewish historian Josephus, writing about AD 100, describes a Jewish lyre of ten strings, played with a plectrum (*Antiquities* VII, 306). This agrees with what we know of the history of lyres. Through the influence of West Semites, a type predominated which was easily played in processions. It was held with the strings horizontal, so that they could be easily swept with a plectrum in the right hand while the left damped unwanted notes (Fig. 6). The *kinnor* is the only instrument of which the sound is characterized for us in the Psalms. It was felt to be *na-im*, 'sweet, lovely' (81.2),

Fig. 6 Semitic lyrist

and it produced a *higgayon*, 'resonance, vibrant murmur' (92.3).

This was the instrument which the traditional father of psalm-singing himself played with great skill, for David is said to have been selected as a youth to play it to King Saul whenever the evil spirit troubled him. He coaxed the spirit away and refreshed and healed the king, playing 'with his hand' (1 Sam. 16.23); this may refer to a softer, more mysterious way of playing with the fingers instead of the sharper plectrum (Fig. 7). This was the instrument, too,

Fig. 7 Lyrist from Megiddo

which the psalm-singers in the Babylonian Exile hung up on the river-side poplars (137.2), as it was not a situation where the songs of Zion, the songs of the Lord, should be sung. This gives us the impression of an easily handled instrument, characteristic of the psalm-singers, and the regular accompani-

75

ment of the hymns expressing joy in the majesty of the Lord and his presence in Zion; there was a time of lament when its voice was silent for grief, but the player would not part with it, for all the hundreds of miles of the march into exile.

The light sweet tones could be effectively combined with other instruments such as larger strings and drums:

> Make music and sound the drums,
> sweet lyres combined with harps!

(81.2)

A company of lyre and harp players walked in the great festal procession behind the singers and flanked by girls with hand-drums (68.25).

It is the Hebrew *nebel* which is here identified as a harp. The harp is well-known in Mesopotamian and Egyptian remains but not in Palestinian, which are in any case rather scanty. But the balance of arguments favours the identification 'harp'. The angular variety depicted on Assyrian reliefs may be our best guide to the Israelite instrument (Fig. 8). An arm joins the end of the sound-box at about a right-angle. The strings, numbering between eight and twenty-two, run diagonally from the arm to the box and so progress evenly from shorter to longer. The instrument was easily played on the move, one variety being held with the strings vertical and so played with the fingers, while another kind was held horizontally and played with a plectrum like a short stick. In the Psalms the *nebel* is sometimes said to have ten strings (33.2; 144.9), while Josephus knew a form with twelve strings played with the fingers. The contexts show that the Israelite *nebel* could be carried and played in processions and that it blended well in the music of praise and testimony (81.2; 33.2) and in the musical ecstasy of prophets (1 Sam. 10.5). Some were made, along with lyres, of a fine imported wood for the use of the singers by order of Solomon (1 Kings 10.12).

Fig. 8 Harpist from Elam

The pipes

It was appreciated in the ancient Near East that the peculiar
colours of the pipe family – flutes, clarinets and oboes –
combined well with the music of the strings. In one instance,
an Assyrian sculptor of the seventh century BC has left us a fine
relief of an Elamite marching band celebrating the installation
of a new king at the behest of the Assyrian conqueror. Fifteen
male and female singers are accompanied by seven vertical
harps, two double oboes, one horizontal harp and one drum.
The double oboe had become generally the preferred wind
instrument by the biblical period and is likely to have been
used in Israel (Fig. 9). Its two pipes of hollow cane are held
downwards from the mouth and diverging a little from each

Fig. 9 Egyptian with double oboe

other. Into each was inserted a double vibrating reed. The pipes were blown together. The right one usually had more finger-holes and supplied the melody, while the left provided droning notes.

An instrument in the orchestra of Psalm 150, the *ugab* (150.4; cf. Gen. 4.21), is probably of the pipe family, to judge by the Targum's Aramaic translation (*abbuba*) and the sound of the word (the root is used of sensuous love). Of this family too is the *halil* (='pierced, hollowed'), which is not actually mentioned in the Psalms, though a similar word (*nehilot*) is used in the heading of Psalm 5. The *halil*-pipes were played as

78

the pilgrims ascended to Zion (Isa. 30.29) and with harp, lyre and drum for the prophets (1 Sam. 10.5). The playing of pipes in the temple is mentioned in the Mishna (*Arakhin* 2.3).

Percussion
One of the most eloquent of instruments, in its own way, is the drum, demanding of its player great talent and knowledge. Several varieties, generally played by hand, are portrayed in the neighbouring countries. The rules for the making and playing of the large, standing, goblet-shaped drum of Babylonian temples bring home to us the awe in which a holy musical instrument might be held. Another huge drum was circular and needed three musicians for its carrying and playing. More easily played in processions were the Assyrian funnel-shaped drum fastened at the player's belt and the Egyptian barrel drum slung across the stomach from the neck. But the most frequently attested drum is the small frame-drum, where skin is stretched over a ring of wood or metal. The player often dances and holds it up in the left hand, tapping it with the right (Fig. 10).

This clearly is the kind of instrument usually denoted by the Hebrew word *top*. Tapping the varied notes of such a drum, the young women danced lithely in the procession of the Lord (Ps. 68.25; cf. Exod. 15.20). Here and in other vivid scenes (1 Sam. 10.5; 2 Sam. 6.5), it added to the other instruments its moving eloquence and rhythm, evoking the magical unity of the group's dance and chorus.

Percussion instruments among early peoples are a large family, an orchestra in themselves. In addition to drums we meet many kinds of devices to give effects of knocking, tinkling, rustling, – kinds of castanets, clappers, clackers, sistra, cymbals and the like. When David brought in the ark, there were players of 'shakers' (*mena-an-im*), and – if the Hebrew text is correct – bars of fir-wood, and cymbals (*selselim*; 2 Sam. 6.5). The shakers may have been related to the Egyptian sistrum, a small metal frame with loose bars, held and shaken from a handle. In Egyptian festivals a row of girls would shake the sistrum with one hand and a collar of pearl

Fig. 10 Egyptians with small-frame drums

strings, called the *Menat*, in the other (Fig. 11); both items were of great symbolic importance, being understood to shake out blessings of life and healing. They sometimes symbolize the whole range of sacred music and dance. David's wooden bars may have been like the boomerang-shaped clackers of Egypt and Mesopotamia, held at the centre, one in each hand, and struck together at top and bottom for varied notes.

While the shakers and batons are not mentioned in the Psalms, the cymbals are, and apparently in two kinds. Psalm 150 calls for praise from *selselim* (root *salal* 'to tingle, quiver') in two phrases which Coverdale renders as 'well-tuned cym-

Fig. 11 Egyptians with shakers

bals' and 'loud cymbals'. The first phrase might rather mean 'cymbals for proclamation', such as might be struck before announcements; in the festal scene this could refer to the proclamation of the coming of God in majesty and salvation. The second phrase may be rendered 'cymbals for acclamation', such as might join the trumpet blasts and shouts acclaiming God's coming in the festival. As it happens, two main designs of cymbals are known in the ancient Near East, the first where two flat plates of bronze are struck together sideways, the second where one bronze cone is clashed downwards on another.

Trumpets and horns
This linking of the quivering clashes and chimes of the cymbals with announcements and acclamations of God's triumph leads us to further musical colour provided on those great occasions by instruments that were more in the nature of signals, albeit of impressive sound. Such was the *hasosera*, the clarion or trumpet with straight slender tube and flared end,

made of metal such as beaten silver (Num. 10.2). In this case, for once, a clear depiction of a Jewish instrument has survived, for it is represented in the captive procession on the arch of Titus in Rome. Josephus (*Antiquities* III. 291) describes a shorter Jewish trumpet, and this accords with the type used in Egypt, such as one played jubilantly by a negro in a festal procession as his companions dance with clubs, or those beautiful trumpets that were recovered from Tutankhamun's tomb. The Israelite trumpets may then have had the surprisingly dark tone that we hear from those of Tutankhamun. Still, they were well adapted to arrest the attention and warn of a great event, and so they join with the other instruments in Psalm 98.6 to announce and then celebrate the coming of God in the festal hour.

Even more impressive was the voice of the *shopar*, the horn of a wild goat or ram, the only instrument allowed in the rites of the later synagogue. This produces a blare of great carrying power, rather like the awesome foghorn. For the favourite phrase 'the voice of the *shopar*' we must note that 'voice' in Hebrew (*qol*) sometimes denotes a powerful sound such as thunder. The *shopar* did sometimes seem like a voice from a higher world, and in the description of God's appearing on Mount Sinai the prelude of lightning and thunder indicates also the voice of a *shopar* of mysterious origin and rising in fearful crescendo:

> And it happened on the third day, when morning broke, that thunder came, and lightnings and heavy cloud over the mountain and a very mighty voice of a *shopar*, and all the people in the camp trembled ... and Mount Sinai smoked all over because the Lord descended upon it in fire ... and the voice of the *shopar* became ever more mighty, as Moses spoke and God answered him by voice.
> (Exod. 19.16–19)

The carrying power of the instrument made it ideal for signalling events across the country. The framework of sacred seasons depended on the sightings of the moon, and the first appearance of the crescent for new-year's day was especially signalled and acclaimed (Num. 29.1). The blowing of the horn on this day is associated with the other music joyfully recognizing the coming of God in his congregation in Psalm 81.3. It is a difficult verse to interpret, with references to both new and full moon. Perhaps this is the sense:

Blow the horns as for the new moon,
as for full moon, on the day of our festival!

The linking of the signalling instruments with the others is more clearly attested in Psalm 47. The horns have signalled the going up of God in triumph and now merge with the response of clapping and singing and playing.

Singers
The voices of the instruments join closely with the human voices. One can almost say that music was song. There was a close partnership of voices and instruments, all applying their strength to the same purposes of proclamation, praise, prayer and teaching. As in much Asian and African music today, the instruments will generally have duplicated the vocal line, adding preludes, intervals and postludes, ornamenting the solo voice and accentuating the rhythm of group singing. Sustained notes of drone harmony were used, and perhaps a kind of two-part harmony.

The voices themselves sounded with their own varieties of mood and colour. The expressive soloist (cf. Fig. 12) would no doubt take the main share of the many psalms formed as utterances of an individual, and probably also in the psalms speaking for the community. Occasionally there are traces of the soloist giving the lead and then calling in the massed voices:

If the Lord had not fought for us
– now let Israel say –
if the Lord had not fought for us
when men rose up against us. . .

(124.1f.)

83

Fig. 12 Singer from Elam beats
her throat to produce tremolo

The interchange of choir and soloist may be traced where a
refrain with 'our' alternates with a passage with 'I':

> O Lord our Lord,
> how glorious is your name in all the world. . .
> When I look at your heavens. . .
> O Lord our Lord. . .

(8.1f.)

Some simple lines with strong rhythm were meant, at the
prompting of the soloist, to be taken up not only by the
disciplined temple choir but by all the pilgrims:

Give thanks to the Lord for he is good!
 Faithful for ever is he!
Let Israel say,
 Faithful for ever is he!
Let the house of Aaron say,
 Faithful for ever is he!
Let those who fear the Lord say,
 Faithful for ever is he!

(118.1ff.)

Or the soloist may call 'Bless the Lord!' and the multitudes
reply 'Blessed be the Lord!' (135.19f.). The common Halleluia originated as such a prompting call, literally 'Praise ye
the Lord!', even if it then became a congregational shout
(106.48). The threefold cry 'Holy' in Isaiah 6.3 reflects
antiphonal singing where 'one kept calling to the other' to and
fro. Similar repetitive chanting is reflected in Psalm 8.1, where
we should probably find the verb 'to repeat' (*tana*, RSV
'chant'); the theme of the exchange here is the Lord's 'glory',
and the use of a short cry for this is indicated in another psalm:
'All in his temple cry Glory!' (29.9). Such chanting with
prostration will be what the same psalm means by 'ascribing
glory to the Lord' (29.1–2). The voices of all the congregation
would especially unite in the word of assent 'Amen' ('truly',
Deut. 27.15f.; Ps.41.13; 72.19; 106.48).
 Phrases like 'Victory is the Lord's' (3.8) and 'The Lord is
King!' may have been taken up by the massed assembly as
part of the triumph cry (*teru-a*), a jubilant acclamation by
voice and instrument of the self-revealing Lord:

All peoples, clap your hands,
acclaim God with ringing cries. . .
God has ascended amidst acclamation,
the Lord with the voice of the horn!

(47.1,5)

Sing to the Lord a new song,
play your utmost on the strings with acclamation!

(33.3)

The impressive guttural sounds of early Hebrew would be present in these martial celebrations of the Lord's triumph:

> The high praises of God be in their throat
> and a two-edged sword in their hand!
>
> (149.6)

We have the impression of two starkly contrasting styles. These were the moods of praise and lament. For praise there was lively rhythm and ringing tones and all the emphasis of supple throat muscles (cf. 47.1). Terms for praise and rejoicing suggest vigorous activity where singing naturally goes with gesture and dance. For lament the singers called and cried to God 'with the voice of groaning', pouring out the plaintive story of woe before him (102 title). There was much growling and moaning and vibrant murmuring (77.3; Isa. 59.11). For lament, no less than for praise, a good volume might be raised, all the better to gain the attention of heaven:

> From deepest regions I call to you, Lord!
> Lord, listen to my voice!
> Let your ears be attentive
> to the noise of my supplication!
>
> (130.1–2)

How great was the sound on one peculiar occasion when the two styles mingled together!

> When the builders laid the foundation of the Lord's temple, the priests in vestments took their positions with trumpets and the Levites, the sons of Asaph, with cymbals to praise the Lord as David, king of Israel, had directed. And they sang responsively with praise and thanksgiving to the Lord: 'Good is he! Faithful for ever is he to Israel!' And all the people shouted the acclamations loudly, praising the Lord because the house of the Lord had been founded again. But many ... who had seen the former temple ... were wailing with loud voices ... so

86

that the people could not distinguish the sound of the joyful acclamation from the sound of the wailing ... and the noise was heard a great way off.

(Ezra 3.10f.)

Specialist women singers were much valued in Israelite society. We hear of them as skilled mourners (2 Chr. 35.25) and as one of the delights of the palace (2 Sam. 19.35). They were included in the tribute sent to appease the Assyrian conqueror in 701 BC. The assembly of returning exiles included two hundred singers, male and female (Ezra 2.65). As regards the religious services, it seems that at least in the period of the monarchy skilled female voices added their contribution. Tradition after all had no difficulty in picturing the sister of Moses as a prophetess whose solo voice led the hymn (Exod. 15.21). The prophetess Deborah was likewise remembered for her mighty hymn (Judg. 5.1). The young women with hand-drums in the procession of Psalm 68.25 complement the male singers and string-players and may well be related to that company of female singers in the assembly of returning exiles. Female singers were prominent in Egyptian religion. Like the male singers, they seem to have rendered a part-time service in the cult. Israelite festal singing would gain greatly in brilliancy of tone from such female voices and better represent the whole voice of humanity.

Notation and musical systems

While the correct performance of music in the ancient Near East was no doubt chiefly handed down orally from person to person, there is some evidence of written directions or notation. Musical terms and instructions, which have not yet been explained, are sometimes found written beside Sumerian liturgies. Explanations have been offered, however, of Babylonian tablets giving the names of nine strings on lyre or harp and of intervals used in tuning. From the method of tuning and retuning it appears that there was a seven-step scale and seven octave-series (distinguished by the position of the semitone) like those of the later Greeks; one of the octave-series is like our major scale. The same musical terms in adapted form appear at the Syrian coastal city of Ugarit, where tablets have been found giving the words of hymns in the Hurrian language, followed by the musical instructions. A plausible and attractive reconstruction of this music has been made, played on a lyre and sung. In the second millennium, then, a common musical system stretched from Mesopotamia to the Mediterranean. The art was revered, its theory deeply understood, and we should not have found it altogether strange.

In the case of the Psalms, hopes of recovering the original music have sometimes been attached to the system of accents which is found throughout the Hebrew Bible, including the Psalms, whereby each word is provided with one of more than twenty signs. The general view, however, has been that this notation originated later than the sixth century AD under the influence of Greek systems, as a detailed guide to phrasing, stresses, and the rise and fall of the voice in reading, and that only later was it linked with the musical phrases of cantors. When lists of the musical value of these signs were eventually drawn up, the values varied from one part of the Bible to another and from one Jewish community to another. Nevertheless, some students continue to hope that these accents preserve a secret from antiquity. Comparisons have been made between the most primitive Jewish and Christian singing known. Between Gregorian chants and Oriental Jewish melodies some resemblances have been observed and thought to point to music received by early Christians from the Jews. In a recent reconstruction by Suzanne Haïk Vantoura, based rather on a fresh decipherment of the accents, the Psalms are sung to austere melodies in a small compass of notes. The soul of the music, of course, would be expressed only with the full animation of emotional colour and dynamics.

Secrets about the musical rendering of the Psalms may also be hidden in various technical expressions found in the Hebrew headings. From attempts to interpret these come supposed names of tunes, references to modes, octaves, choirmasters and the like in our English Bibles and commentaries. The heading of Psalm 22, for example, is rendered in RSV: 'To the choir-master, according to (the tune) "Hind of the dawn"'. Such interpretations are mostly far from secure.

The recovery of the specific original music of the Psalms is bound to be a daunting task. The survey we have made, however, shows something of the effects of that music in the souls of the ancient worshippers. Through their ears we can share in the moods and colours of the eloquent instruments and voices. And certainly, the growing knowledge of ancient Near Eastern music seizes our attention and fills us with respect for the ancient musicians. It is clear that we are in the presence of master artists, who in varying moods of contemplation, ecstasy, lament and joy addressed their art to the Holy One.

Music as inspired

We turn now from the means of music to the meaning of music in the Psalms. Towards the end of the Old Testament period, the writer of Chronicles described how he believed King David had made provision for music and singing in the temple; David had set apart those 'who should *prophesy* with lyres, harps and cymbals' (1 Chr. 25). The music was thus seen as an inspired art, prompted by the spirit of God, pouring forth its peculiar utterance in close contact with God. When David came to be seen as the chief author of the Psalms, there would be no difficulty in thinking of him as inspired like a prophet. His inspiration is emphasized in the composition recorded as his last words in 2 Samuel 23:

> The oracle of the man the High One raised,
> the anointed of the God of Jacob,
> sweetest singer of Israel:
> The spirit of the Lord speaks by me,
> his word is upon my tongue. . .

There are also some psalms attributed to other prophets or seers, such as Moses (Ps. 90), Heman (Ps. 88) and Habakkuk

89

(Hab. 3). A considerable number of psalms contain 'oracles', where words of God are mediated in the first person (e.g. 50.5,7f.; 81.6f.; 95.8f.). One psalm begins with a vivid description of inspiration:

> My heart seethes with a good message,
> I must utter my poem for the king,
> my tongue (fast-driven) as the pen of a rapid scribe.
>
> (45.1)

Moreover, the festal celebration with instruments and singing is taken to be an appointment of God (81.1–5). The rejoicing is brought about by God (86.4; 90.14–15; 92.4); he puts the song into the singer's mouth (40.3).

The divine origin of music was a common idea in the ancient world. In Egypt, for example, it was expressed in the personification of music as the goddess Mert.

Music as an offering
While music is then, in a sense, from the Lord, it is also for the Lord. The temple music is not designed for the pleasure of the worshippers, but for him who is worshipped. Expressions for praising the Lord and giving thanks to him are constantly linked with those for playing and singing:

> We will sing and play of your might.
>
> (21.13)

> I will thank you, Lord, with all my heart,
> I will recount all your miracles,
> I will be glad and exult in you,
> I will make music to your name, O Most High.
>
> (9.1–2)

> With my song I give thanks to him.
>
> (28.7)

90

Give thanks to the Lord with the lyre,
with the ten-stringed harp make music to him,
sing to him a new song,
harp skilfully with acclamations!

(33.2–3)

I will thank you with the lyre, O God my God.

(43.4)

With every instrument and every breath praise is to be offered before the revelation of the Lord (Ps.150).

As the ancient language of sacrifice spoke of the incense and smoke rising pleasantly to God's senses, so the music too should sound sweet to him:

I will sing to the Lord through all my life,
I will make music to my God while I have being.
May my composition be sweet to him,
while I rejoice in the Lord!

(104.33–4)

The words from the singer's lips, and still more the music of his heart which is resounding like his lyre, are to be for 'favour', finding acceptance and grace before the Lord:

May the utterance of my mouth
and the sounding of my heart
rise before you for favour,
Lord, my rock and redeemer!

(19.14)

Thanksgiving was expressed through sacrifices along with acclaim of God's triumph and the music of psalmody:

And now shall my head be raised
above my enemies round about me,
that I may sacrifice in his tent
sacrifices with acclamation.
I will sing and make music to the Lord.

(27.6)

When vows were fulfilled with the offering of beasts, a song of testimony recounted the story of God's help (66.13ff.). It could be said that the song delighted God more than did the offered beast:

> I will praise God's name with song
> and extol it with thanksgiving,
> and this will please the Lord more than an ox,
> more than a bull perfect in horn and hoof.

> (69.30–31)

We may say, then, that the music of worship, comprehending instruments and voices and expressing praise and testimony, is itself an offering to God. A similar notion in the surrounding countries may again be illustrated from Egyptian art. Offerings and prayers are shown as presented with playing or offering of the sistrum, representing all the music and dance of worship.

The music of the universe
We find a greater depth of meaning in the musical praise of God when we observe that it is the counterpart of music in heaven. God's ascension and revelation of his glory are taken to be a cosmic event, only reflected in miniature at Zion's temple. The heavenly beings bow low before him and ascribe majesty to him with antiphonal hymns acknowledging his glory and holiness (8; 29; Isa. 6). The temple's music is joined to this mighty praise, in which all species of living things are bidden to take part (148; 150). The theme on earth is the same as that in heaven:

> The Lord is King!
> Holy is he!
> Holy is he!
> The Lord our God is holy!

> (99.1,3,5,9)

The praising music is a symphony in which all, above and below, play their part: angels, sun, moon, stars, the heavens, the ocean above the sky, the earth and creatures of land and sea and air, fire, hail, snow, frost, wind, mountains, all peoples, the old and the young (148). All make music to the Lord in their own way: while men sing and play lyres and trumpets, the sea roars, the floods clap, the mountains give echoing cry before the Lord (98.5–9).

Such universal praise is not only the acclaim which acknowledges the sole glory of the Lord. It includes testimony. Without human language, the elements of the cosmos are yet able to pass on their narration of the deeds of God. They are eloquent with holy knowledge imparted to them from the mysteries of God, and as they chant it one to another, the fellowship of creation gains power to live and continue. This is a music more essential to life than air or water:

> The heavens are telling the glory of God
> and the sky-vault declares the deeds of his hands,
> each day pours out utterance to the next
> and one night to another expounds the knowledge.
> They use no earthly phrase or word,
> their voice is not for human ears,
> but their music rings through all the earth
> and to the bounds of the world go their words.
>
> (19.1f.)

Here the climaxes of praise link with a continuity. The moment of the great revelation of God, when he ascends and manifests himself in royal glory and is acclaimed King in heaven and earth, the high moment in fact of the temple's festivals, is really the focus of a continuing praise in which all the created order ever refreshes itself.

The close sympathy of the temple's music and the great elements of nature appears in another connection, when, with the passing of a night of supplication, the singer calls awake his soul and his instruments, that they in turn may waken the angel of morning, and the world may be filled with testimony:

93

Awake, my glory!
Awake, harp and lyre!
I will waken the dawn.
I will praise you among the peoples, Lord,
I will make music to you among the nations,
for your fidelity stands high as the heavens
and your truth reaches up to the clouds.

(57.8–10)

The musical praise of God, which thus unites all creatures,
must therefore reconcile warring nations:

Kingdoms of the earth, sing to God,
make music to the Lord!

(68.32)

From the rising of the sun to its setting
let the name of the Lord be praised!

(113.3)

Musical praise as communion with God

While the songs of praise treat the deeds and attributes of
God, they do so the better to attain their real subject, God
himself. The most direct way for the singers to set their minds
and the minds of their hearers on God himself is to chant his
name, the awesome name in which they experience his person
and presence:

With (chanting of) his name 'Yah' exult before him!

(68.4)

So shall I play and sing your name for ever,
fulfilling my vows every day.

(61.8)

Give thanks to the Lord,
proclaim his name,
declare among the peoples his deeds,

94

> sing to him, make music to him,
> celebrate with chanting of his holy name!

(105.1f.)

With such chanting, the name of God constitutes the content of the song, and it is but a short step to say that the music's meaning is the Lord himself:

> My glory and my music is Yah.

(118.14)

In keeping with this understanding of the music's meaning is the ancient practice of the Church in singing the 'Jubilus': the last syllable of the Alleluia (Yah, the Hebrew name of God) is dwelt on with many notes and beautiful phrases.

We considered earlier the music of acclamation, the music and vocal formulas which salute God's coming. In paying such tribute to his presence, the worshippers dispose themselves towards him. They acknowledge that the glory and the godhead are his and that they themselves are his dependent creatures:

> The Lord alone is God,
> he it is who made us
> and to him we belong,
> his people and the flock of his pasture.

(100.3)

Thus the worshippers are led to concentrate on him; all their thoughts and their wonder are absorbed in him. It is an experience of communion. Sometimes, indeed, the music of acclamation is at once followed by the speech of the Lord to his worshippers (81; 95). Thus, both with the music of acclamation or praise and that of testimony or thanksgiving, the singers and listeners are drawn to rapt contemplation of God. The music takes on an ecstatic quality. It has lifted the worshippers into awareness of reality, into an inexpressible experience of the divine.

Music as enlightenment

While such significance of the music is easier to trace in the words of the holy songs, the role of the instruments is yet of great importance. The voices of the horn, the lyre, and all their fellows are thought to pass readily to and from the heavens. As David had controlled an evil spirit with his lyre (1 Sam. 16.14f.) and Elisha had gained knowledge from above through the playing of a harp or lyre (2 Kings 3.15), so the psalmist will strain his ear to catch secrets from beyond, playing his lyre to unlock the darkest puzzles of life:

> I will incline my ear for a parable,
> with the lyre I will unlock my riddle.
>
> (49.4)

In those psalms which are addressed not to God but to men, their music lends inspired force. Teaching must wrestle with great difficulties – dullness of mind and heart in teacher and taught, and the baffling nature of life's problems. With his music the teacher becomes a prophet and things from beyond are given him to utter, flowing sentences of truth and power:

> Listen, my people, to my teaching,
> incline your ear to the utterance of my mouth!
> I will open my mouth in parables,
> I will pour forth mysteries from of old.
>
> (78.1–2)

Such teaching is both new and old, new revelation and still old tradition:

> things that we have heard and known,
> that our fathers recounted to us.
>
> (78.3)

The old topics treated, such as the lessons of history, were always liable to be misunderstood or ignored, and ever fresh inspiration must come to teachers and hearers alike.

96

The piety of devotion to God's law, so characteristic of later Judaism, had already begun to develop in the period of the Psalms. Music naturally has its place in such psalms as are offerings of praise and prayer to God in appreciation of his laws (19.14; 119.7,62,108,164,169f.). But the recitation of laws as part of this piety seems also to have tended to a musical chant, foreshadowing the later Jewish practice of intoning all scripture:

> Songs have your statutes become for me
> in the house where I sojourn.

> (119.54)

Words usually rendered 'meditate' (*haga*) and 'muse' (*siah*) probably denote a kind of intoned recitation:

> His delight is in the law of the Lord
> and from his law he intones day and night.

> (1.2)

> How I love your law!
> It is my chant all the day long.

> (119.97)

And so we would see again how music is the medium for illuminating words from beyond, and words which are offered again to God.

Music that pleads

That music readily passes from and to the heavenly realm makes its use appropriate in lamenting supplication. As we have already noted, its tone is quite different in lamentation. Some instruments may have been left aside, hung up in silent eloquence, while others, such as pipes, may still have been used in mournful style. From the dishevelled worshippers rose a pathetic 'voice of groaning', a moaning and a vibrant murmuring. Still, it was music of a kind, sometimes led by a priestly choir (Joel 2.17) and carrying the appeal movingly to God's ears. So God-given music, like the Holy Spirit of which

St Paul speaks (Rom. 8.26), prays with the sufferers in language surpassing speech.

Most psalms of lament include passages in more cheerful mood, anticipating God's merciful response. Here the varied eloquence of music would play its part, suddenly irradiating the scene with the light and colour of hope.

God's Son as the chief minstrel

For the meaning of music in the Psalms, there is some importance in its association with the office of king. The royal calling is treated with such depth in the Psalms that it becomes in many ways a foreshadowing of the office of Messiah. In Psalm 45, for example, the wedding of a king is raised by the psalmist to prophetic glory. The very sovereignty of God is seen to be mediated through the king's office: his throne is as God's, enduring for ever in the cause of right (45.6). Amidst these weighty statements, we hear that God himself has now anointed the king; as his bride stands beside him, his robes flow with the fragrant oil. Associated with this mighty sacrament is music. For this anointed of God is now filled with joy by music of lyres and harps which reaches him in the court from within the palace rooms. The music bears a heavenly blessing and invites him to enter with his bride for the consummation by which the royal line shall be continued and the work of God extended:

> Your throne, the throne of God,
> is for ever and ever,
> the sceptre of right is the sceptre of your kingship.
> You have loved right and opposed wrong,
> and so God, your God, has anointed you
> above your fellows with the oil of gladness.
> Myrrh, aloes and cassia flow on your garments,
> from palace rooms panelled with ivory
> stringed instruments fill you with joy. . .
> Instead of your fathers shall be your sons,
> you shall appoint them as governors through all the earth.
> (45.6–8,16)

But often in the Psalms kings appear as themselves musicians. In the tradition of David, they are supposed to take the lead in using instrument and song to praise and thank God, to bear witness to him and instruct the people:

> O God, a new song I will sing for you,
> with a ten-stringed harp I will make music for you
> as giver of salvation to the kings,
> deliverer of David your servant.
>
> (144.9–10)

It is part of the calling of David and his heirs that they stand as witnesses for the Lord to all the nations (Isa.55.4), and they bear their testimony through instrument and song:

> And so I will confess you, Lord, among the nations
> and I will make music to your name
> as the God who works great salvation for his king
> and fulfils his promises to his anointed,
> to David and his seed for ever.
>
> (18.49–50)

Although the association of David with most of the psalms is partly a later development, it is likely that psalms of or for kings always formed a vital part of the collection. The king's office is thus a major theme of the Psalms. The royal figure emerges as an ideal, the representative who sings the song of suffering and salvation, being raised from the depths to the heights. He foreshadows the Messiah as the one whom God brings to shine with the divine glory and mediate God's rule. And it is in keeping with the deep and holy meaning of music in the Psalms that this chosen servant and son is also the chief musician, the foremost minstrel, leading the world in songs of praise and prayer and testimony.

The music of life
For the most part the Psalms express that stage of biblical religion where the abode of the dead, Sheol, was thought of as

the opposite of the land of the living. Belief in the rising again to life of the individual dead had yet to develop. The last state of human beings was seen as a persistence of ghostly shadows in a subterranean cavern without light or sound. Here was no music:

> The dead do not praise the Lord,
> none who go down into the silence.

(115.17)

The music of testimony had no place there; nothing was heard, seen, or remembered:

> For the dead will you work miracles
> or will the shades stand up to give you thanks?
> Is your faithful dealing recounted in the grave,
> your faithfulness in the land of the lost?
> Are your marvels known in the darkness
> or your salvation where all is forgotten?

(88.10–12)

The forces of faith and hope had thus to be channelled within the bounds of this life, breaking forth in the recovery of a person's health and joy and in the renewal of families and communities. The opportunities on earth for life were all the more treasured, and life in its richest form was experienced in the music of praise before the Lord. Led by all the instruments and singers and dancers, every creature that had the breath of life should here drink that cup of life to the full in praising the glorious Creator:

> Praise God in his sanctuary!
> Praise him in the sky-vault that shines with his splendour!
> Praise him with telling of his mighty deeds!
> Praise him for the greatness of his power!
> Praise him with blast of horns!
> Praise him with harps and lyres!
> Praise him with hand-drums and whirling dances!

100

Praise him with strings and pipes!
Praise him with cymbals for proclamation!
Praise him with cymbals for acclamation!
Every breathing thing, praise the Lord!
All of you, praise the Lord!

(150)

5

DANCING AND THE PSALMS

If music has generally held an honoured position in the history of worship, the same can hardly be said for dancing. The art was often banished from the churches. As prominently physical, it might be considered unsuited to times of spiritual and mental reflection; as sensuous, it might be feared as awakening sexual feelings. And so the joy of worship had to be experienced inwardly or at most with singing. Ministers entered and departed with leaden tread, their feet restrained to the minimal role of conveyance. Worshippers were chained to the pews with heavy inhibitions, rising only to sing the prescribed hymns with the aid of books and spectacles. During the present century, various influences have been at work to modify this situation. The dangers of denying the body its proper role have been stressed. The profound meanings of dance have been explored. The exhilaration of worship in non-European traditions has made its impact. But whatever the source of influence or line of argument, the advocates of dance in worship have a weighty ally in the Old Testament, and in particular in the Psalms.

Dancing often taken for granted
Dancing before God was such a natural activity of worship for the people of the Old Testament that it scarcely called for mention or description. Often, when the worshippers are pictured rejoicing and making merry before God, it seemed to the author superfluous to specify that they danced. 'How else does one rejoice?' he might have answered us. Occasionally we

have stories which confirm this point; the scene is first described as a 'rejoicing' and then later the turn of the story happens to require that the act of dancing be specified. Thus, at David's first attempt to bring in the ark, he and all the people are described as 'rejoicing (*sahaq*) before the Lord' to the playing of strings, drums, shakers and cymbals (2 Sam. 6.5). A sinister event caused the ceremony to be suspended for some months. When it was resumed, the scene again was one of 'rejoicing' (*simha*), but the detail of the king's dance is now added to prepare for the comment of his wife Michal, who disparaged his dancing and consequently remained childless (2 Sam. 6.14f.). In another famous story, the 'merry-making' (*sahaq*) before the golden calf comes dramatically into focus as the puzzled Moses draws near: he sees 'dances' (Exod. 32.6,19).

Another word usually rendered 'rejoice' (*gil*) has been compared with a similar Arabic word 'to turn round and round' and an Ethiopic word 'to dance and sing', and in one occurrence the Jerusalem Bible bodly renders it 'dance', thus portraying God himself as a dancer:

> Yahweh your God is in your midst,
> a victorious warrior.
> He will exult with joy over you,
> he will renew you by his love;
> he will dance with shouts of joy for you
> as on a day of festival.
>
> (Jerusalem Bible, Zeph. 3.17)

Such an idea would not be strange in the Hebrew tradition. In one profound passage, God's creative thought, 'Wisdom', the divine order in the world, is portrayed as a girl who ever delights him with her dancing and playing ('rejoicing', *sahaq*) as he established the universe (Prov. 8.30). In much later times a Jewish exposition of the Song of Songs declares (with reference to Psalm 48.13–14) that God will lead the dance among the righteous in the new age (Midrash *Shir* 7,1). The same passage interprets various biblical stories of angels as heavenly dances, for example Genesis 32.1–2: 'Sixty myriads of angels danced and leapt before our father Jacob when he went out from the house of Laban'.

The vision of God dancing is rich in meaning. It speaks of his dynamic nature, his relation to the physical world, his sharing in the joy of his creatures, and his commitment to the triumph of joyful love. It is interesting too that heavenly dance is a theme found among other peoples. In Phoenicia there was a god known as 'Lord of the Dance' (*baal marqod*), Egypt had dancing deities, while in India it is the deity Shiva above all who is portrayed in dancing posture and known as 'Lord of the Dance'.

There is another interesting Hebrew word which can imply dancing: the verb 'to prophesy', that is, 'act the prophet'. In our chapter on music, it was noted how the work of psalm-singers could be called 'prophesying'. There are passages depicting groups of prophets engaged in a 'prophesying' which takes the form of infectious music and dancing in communion with God. The picture of this activity emerges from several stories (1 Sam. 10.5; 19.20f.; 1 Kings 18.19f.; 22.10), and there are parallels in the Islamic dervishes. The prophets move in orderly formation to the tapping of drums and playing of pipes and plucked strings, and with chanting of the name and attributes of God. These corporate exercises are maintained for long periods and result in an experience of ecstasy or seizure by the divine spirit, and so bring the possibility of an oracle. An appropriate occasion for such prophesying was at the sanctuary in the festal season. The prophets' dancing is of interest as showing in a particular form the nature of dance as communion, seeking and enjoying the spirit of God, sharing the experience in a brotherly fellowship and leading to a message for the wider circle.

Terms for dancing
The specific words for dancing give further impressions of energetic movement. The noun for 'dance' (*mahol, mehola*) comes from the verb meaning 'to whirl, dance, writhe'. Such a dance would be likely to involve spinning and twisting by the individual dancer as well as circling in formation. David's

104

movements in his processional dance before the ark are described in the earlier account as 'spinning, wheeling' (*mekarker*) and 'leaping up and down' (*mepazzez*, 2 Sam. 6.16), while Chronicler depicts him as 'bounding, skipping' (*meraqqed*) and 'making merry, sporting' (*mesaheq*, 1 Chron. 15.29). This dancing 'before the Lord' was 'with all his might' (2 Sam. 6.14) and can be compared with dancing known in various parts of the world where the last ounce of strength is devoted to the dance of divine communion. In Egyptian festivals dancers somersaulted to the rhythm of drums and shakers (Fig. 13). Caitanya, the Indian devotee of Krishna, was often

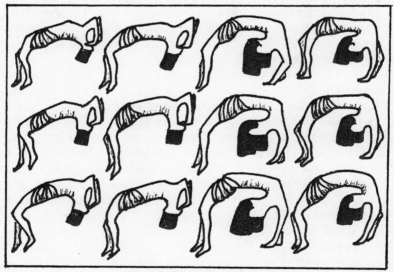

Fig. 13 Egyptian dancers

impelled to express his overpowering love for the deity by singing and dancing the holy dramas like a madman, even to the point of unconsciousness. Of Saul too it is said that, after dancing with Samuel's band of prophets with all the force of the spirit of God upon them, he lay unconscious for many hours (1 Sam. 19.24).

Two other words applied to dancing movements or steps are

105

of interest. A step with a limping or springing action was used by Baal's prophets as they circled his altar to the point of exhaustion (1 Kings 18.26); the verb used of this 'limp' has the same consonants as the name of the great spring festival, the Passover (*pesah*), and some scholars have looked for the origin of the festival's name in a festal dance. A little more solid is the association with dance of another term for a festival, *hag*, which applied especially to the pilgrimage festival of the autumn. In some passages the verb of this root (*hagag*) seems to indicate dancing or circular movement, while a similar root (*hug*) denotes 'circle, ring'. It is possible that a circling dance gave its name to the festival and pilgrimage as a whole. The same word is used in Arabic of the annual pilgrimage feast at Mecca, where the circling of the holy stone is the main rite.

The continuing use of dancing
Dancing is attested as a part of Israel's worship throughout the biblical period and beyond. It was not a primitive exercise which gradually died out. From the end of the era there are reports of dancing preserved in the Mishna. Here (*Taanith* 4.8) we read that a rabbi of the first century AD declared that there were no happier days than those when the maidens of Jerusalem went out in white garments to dance in the vineyards. 'Young man, lift up your eyes and see what you would choose for yourself!' they would sing, immediately adding, 'Set not your eyes on beauty ... let the woman who fears the Lord be praised!' This dance on certain holy days was matched over a thousand years earlier. For an annual event at the sanctuary of Shiloh, during the autumn festival, was the going out of the maidens to dance in the vineyards. In the particular year referred to by Judges 21.19f., the girls were snatched away by liers-in-wait to provide wives for a depleted tribe. One can discern that in normal years the maidens danced with thoughts of marriage as did their Jerusalem counterparts at the end of the era.

A prophecy in Jeremiah reflects a similar custom in the period of the Psalms. In the days of the Exile the prophet foresees the restoration of the great autumn festival. Pilgrims from far and wide will answer the summons 'Arise and let us go to Zion, to the Lord our God' and they will go up the height of Zion and sing aloud in thankfulness for the fertile earth and its produce. Israel is pictured as one of the maidens who dresses herself for the ceremony of the dance and goes out with the merry-makers:

Then maidens shall rejoice in the dance
and young men and old shall be merry.
I will turn their mourning into joy,
I will comfort them
and give them gladness for sorrow.

(Jer. 31.13)

A story of dancing in the late period is found in 3 Maccabees concerning a miraculous deliverance of persecuted Jews in the third century BC: 'They took up the song of their fathers, praising God the saviour of Israel and worker of wonders; putting aside all wailing and lamentation, they formed dances in token of joy for their safe deliverance' (3 Macc. 6.32f.).

Even the ecstatic dancing of the prophetic companies has some counterpart in the late period, though prophetic practices had generally receded. For the Mishna (*Sukka* 5) again reflects scenes at the festival in the first century AD, telling of a remarkable dance in the temple courts when darkness fell after the first day of the autumn feast of Tabernacles. In the Court of the Women stood golden torch-pillars said to be fifty cubits high. Ladders were climbed to fill the oil bowls at the top and the great wicks made of worn-out priestly garments were set ablaze. Numerous Levites with lyres and harps, cymbals and other instruments made music of praise on the fifteen steps that led to the Court of the Israelites. To the fore came 'men of piety and good works' or 'miracle workers' – dervish-like holy men who danced daringly with flaming torches in their hand and chanted praises.

Dancing at the coming of the Lord
When the menfolk of old Israel were called from home to the

107

wars of the Lord, their women would wait in the greatest suspense for news of the battle. All the greater was their rejoicing when the host returned victorious. Wives and daughters went out from the towns and villages to meet them with dances, hand-drums and responsive chants. Such was the scene when Jephthah returned from victory over the Ammonites (Judg. 11.34) and when Saul and David returned from defeating the Philistines (1 Sam. 18.6).

The victory of the Exodus, when the Lord, as a 'man of war', hurled the host of Pharaoh into the sea (Exod. 15) was pictured with a similar scene. It was as though he too marched home to a welcome from the dancing women, for

> Miriam the prophetess took a drum in her hand and all the women went out after her with drums and dances, and Miriam sang to them, 'Sing to the Lord for he has triumphed gloriously; horse and rider he has thrown in the sea!'

This scene of welcome has probably become part of the Exodus story through the custom of re-enacting the story in ceremonies of worship. Processions signified the going forth of the Lord from his sanctuary to defeat evil forces, and his victorious return amid celebrations of music and dance. In the lead are the women prophets, inspired to dance in the near presence of the Lord and to interpret and proclaim his deeds in responsive hymns and bodily movements.

Such a coming in of the Lord to reign victoriously from his sanctuary (Exod. 15.17–18) became a central experience of festal worship. The great Psalm 68 seems to have been sung during such a procession and gives descriptions and explanations of the successive scenes. It is the homeward march of the victorious God, and his presence in the procession is probably signified by his chief symbol, the portable ark, for the beginning of the psalm is like the chant used for the lifting up of the ark (Num. 10.35). Before the face of the Lord go the priestly singers and lyre and harp players. This company is surrounded by young women with hand-drums, who no doubt play in the liturgy the role of the welcoming women. With prophetic powers like the classic figure Miriam, they move in the holy aura of the entering Lord, greeting him and declaring his deeds with songs and dances. The prophetic character of their performance may provide the explanation of the feminine word used in verse 11 for 'tidings-bearers' (*mebasserot*). The procession, as an action of God, waited upon the indication of his will. When he gave the word, authorizing the message of salvation, the procession entered and 'great was the host of women bearing tidings'. So these inspired female dancers mediated the word for the rite, projecting the gospel of God's triumph.

Up the holy mountain went the procession, attaining at last the highest point in the holy of holies, the symbolic throne-room of the Lord where the ark was placed as his footstool. It all signified the ascension of the heavenly King and manifested his supremacy and salvation, as Psalm 47 especially shows. When this ecstatic psalm calls for the clapping of hands and the chants of acclamation and all the music of praise and declares that the Lord, the King, has ascended with the shouts and the voice of the horn, it must be assumed that the scene included dancing. The description of the entry of the ark in 2 Sam. 6 makes this all the more likely, for there too there is an entry and ascension of the Lord in symbol of his ark (vv. 12–17) and a great dancing with drums and shakers and all manner of instruments (vv.5,14).

Dancing for the new age

With the Lord now ascended, the worshippers have entered the holy moment when all is made new. To God the Creator and restorer must be offered 'new' praise, suited to this vision of his new kingdom:

> Sing to the Lord a new song,
> praise for him in the assembly of the faithful!

(149.1)

Dancing expresses joy in the maker and King of all that is, as the whole assembly moves to the beating of the drums:

109

Let Israel rejoice in his maker,
the sons of Zion be joyful in their King!
Let them praise his name with circling dances,
with hand-drums and strings let them make music for
him!

(149.2–3)

Psalm 149 may next disclose another element in the celebration: seated on their mats in the temple court, the worshippers watch sword-dancers enact the defeat of the wicked forces, and they participate with the acclamation of God's triumph (149.4–9).

In calling the festal worshippers 'sons of Zion' this psalm reminds us how the poetry of the festival personified Zion as the bride of God and mother of his people. The precious little Psalm 87 enshrines a beautiful vision of this motherhood, culminating in dance. The Lord who has come with love for his 'Zion' extends his love to all peoples, even those who once opposed him. Seated now in his triumph, he is busy apportioning the destinies for the new era. As he writes up his register of the peoples, he records as mother-city of each one: 'Zion'! In Zion is seen the paradise where all know their Creator and drink of the fountain of life. And what can these reunited and redeemed ones do but dance and sing of the new life which they can find in Zion alone?

And as they dance, they sing
'All my fresh springs are in you'.

(87.7)

Dancing before the ascended Lord is surely to be connected also with the ecstasy of praise that is Psalm 150. His coming into Zion and his ascending there to his reign of glory is a disclosure of his supremacy above all the world. Thus the psalm calls for praise in the immediate presence of the Lord in his sanctuary, yet at the same time above the sky-vault that shines with the glory of his epiphany. The praise is led by the sacred·musicians and dancers of the temple, but it is for all breathing things to join in. The breath gives life and the life is an impulse towards God, a dance to the giver of breath. All manner of things move together in joy around his throne, saying with their dancing bodies as with their lips, 'Halleluia! Praise the Lord!', indeed with their dances taking the message further than words alone could reach.

The Lord's anointed as leader of the dance
It has been already noted that the turn of the story of David in 2 Samuel 6 necessitated the giving of some details as to the king's part in the procession of the Lord to his sanctuary. After the ark had been conveyed six paces, David sacrificed an ox and a fatling. Clad in a priestly apron, the linen ephod, he then began to dance 'before the Lord' (that is, before the advancing ark) with all his might and continued bounding and whirling all the way into the city. It was a leading role, rather than a solo, for the whole people acted together to bring up the ark and 'make merry' (with dancing) with all their might before the Lord (2 Sam. 6.5,15). This great event was foundational and likely to be commemorated with a degree of re-enactment annually. We are told that it was at the autumn festival that Solomon brought the ark into the new temple (1 Kings 8) and this would be the appropriate time ever after to recall the first entry of the Lord into his Jerusalem residence. Psalm 132 then seems to belong to such renewals, showing how later kings pleaded for favour on the strength of David's piety. The locating of the ark by David's men and the beginning of the ark's procession to Jerusalem are clearly re-enacted in the psalm (132.6–7). Dancing is not specified, but there are allusions to the rejoicing and celebration (vv.9, 16f.). That the Davidic kings continued to lead on these great occasions is clear enough in the records (1 Kings 8.5,54f., 62f.; 2 Kings 16.12f; 23.1–3 etc) and the Chronicler portrays the ninth century king Jehoshaphat as leading his men in a procession of rejoicing into the temple (2 Chr. 20.27–8).

It is possible that the lamenting Psalm 42 provides a further illustration, though one cannot be certain that it is the utterance of a king. It would certainly fit a king's role, in the succession of David, when the singer pathetically recalls how in happier times he had led the dancing festal throng:

> I passed into the sanctuary,
> I led them with dancing step up to the house of God
> with the thunder of praise and thanksgiving,
> as the multitude circled in the festal dance.

(42.4)

In Psalm 118 also, it is not spelt out whether the central figure in the psalm's vivid scenes is Israel's king, but there is good reason to assume it. A grand festal setting is indicated by the beginning and end of the psalm, and it is fairly clear that the procession taking place is richly symbolic. Ceremonies have shown that it is the humble whom the Lord exalts. The ruler learns that in himself he is nothing. Only by faith in the Lord can he be saved. So he is led from his trials up through the temple gates as one acceptable to the Lord, fit to be the bonding stone of God's society. But how to express the message of light and life which now irradiates the procession of worshippers – except by dancing? Around the altar in the spacious court before the temple the king leads the circling dance, and the call goes up to 'bind the festal dance with cords up to the horns of the altar' (118.27). The translation 'cords' fits best with the verb 'bind', and such ribbon-like cords will have guided the dancing movement in orderly companies. 'Branches' is an alternative rendering; these symbols of life were in evidence at the festivals and might have been held as links between the dancers and finally with the altar's horns (four spikes rising at the corners), which were treated as specially holy points. Whatever the details, the movement was a bodily expression of the testimony:

> The Lord is God
> and he has caused light to shine on us!

(118.27)

In our previous chapter it was seen how the office of the Davidic kings included the role of God's chief minstrel. Music being such a large part of worship, the chief worshipper must take the lead in playing and singing for God. And now it appears that dancing had a similar dignity. It belonged to the highest expressions of knowledge of God, and the Lord's anointed, chief partner in God's reign, should out-dance all others in the joy of being close to him. The evidence of the Psalms, supported by the historical books, is just clear enough to show this ideal being sustained. Called to be close to the Lord and mediator of his light, the Lord's anointed gives supreme expression to this calling in the dance.

The dance of thanksgiving and testimony

When an Israelite was delivered from some great danger, such as a deadly illness, his chief thought was to go to the temple and acknowledge the salvation before God and men. The youngest of Job's counsellors, the voluble Elihu, describes such a situation: a man becomes so ill that he lies in bed tormented by pain; unable to eat, he wastes away and his bones protrude; he is at the borders of the land of death. But a good angel intercedes for him and eases the way for the man's own prayers. God grants him healing and he makes pilgrimage to the temple to 'see the face of God with acclamation' – that is, to join in the festival where God's glory shines forth and is acclaimed, and life is known at its fullest. No doubt bringing an offering, he testifies before men that God has been merciful to him, a sinner, and has redeemed him from the land of death and bathed him in the light of life (Job 33.19–28). As for the manner of this testimony, one may translate as RSV 'he sings before men'.

A song of this kind is Psalm 30, though it came to be applied to the salvation of the community. Even if it was originally composed for royal use, it no doubt reflects the pattern followed by other citizens. There is here a blend of praising acknowledgement addressed to the Lord and testimony addressed to other worshippers. A time of peace and complacency had been ended with sudden illness. The soul seemed already in the underworld of the dead. But urgent prayer was answered. The Lord brought the soul up again to the land of life; he changed the penitential mourning into dancing and replaced the sackcloth with garments of rejoicing. The saved man comes to the temple with his offering of thanksgiving and tells the story of experienced grace to surrounding worshippers. By his dance at the temple, he enhances his words of thanks and testimony, for his dance is the celebration of life before God, the opposite pole to mourning in the shadow of death. The same pattern can be discerned in the vision of the prophet who saw how the lame man would leap as a hart (Isa. 35.6); we recall also Peter's healing of the lame man, who at once entered the temple, leaping and praising God (Acts 3). It is always natural to leap for joy. To leap and dance before God was the natural way also for the Israelites to thank him for life and testify of his life-restoring forgiveness.

Assessing the dance
Dancing was obviously not a side-show in the religion that produced the Psalms. It was a normal part of the expression of worship in its highest moments. In the climax of the great annual festivals especially, when the community was conscious of the presence of God as Creator and saviour, dancing joined music and singing as a chief means of worship. Hence it was not enough for some professional dancer to put on a show. The Lord's anointed himself must lead the dance, and dance with all his might before the Lord. Sacred personnel indeed played their part, especially the lithe young women with drums and responsive chants; sword-dancers may have enacted scenes; prophets danced in their peculiar inspiration and foreshadowed acts of God. But it was for all Israel to rejoice in the Lord, and for all Israel therefore to dance.

It may be possible to sing hymns and halleluias with an absent mind or a cold heart. It was much harder to dance to the festal drums without involvement. The dancing was thus a wonderful means for every person, from head to toe, to be glad in the Lord. Through the dancing it was all the more likely that all present thoroughly took part in the holy event,

114

the enactment of God's coming and his purifying and renewing his people.

Nor could a dancing worshipper enjoy God in an isolated fashion. His movements were visible. His emotion was shared. The rhythm was common to all, and the joy in God was joy also in the fellowship of his people. From the leading dancers a message in effect was spread: 'Rejoice in the Lord! Turn from self-obsession! He has freed us! With us be glad in him!'

So great was this Lord, so deep this fellowship, that the boundaries of the dancing community went wider and wider. They knew that the trees also clapped their hands, the sea roared and the earth itself danced before the Lord. The pulsing of love and joy in the Lord ran through all that he had made. This was the rhythm of life at its truest, the life of creation in the light of God's face.

Such was the dance in the worship of the psalmists. Those who experienced it might well have asked, 'How could there be worship without dancing?'

6
DRAMA AND THE PSALMS

Under the warm Jerusalem sun, throngs of pilgrims were pressing into the sacred court. Wherever a ledge or a roof afforded a vantage point, the people perched precariously. Custodians of order held the excited crowds back from one or two lanes that led to the centre. Here stood a raised stage, where figures in colourful costumes now began to enact an ancient sacred story. From a high ledge on a wall a priest sang out the narrative framework of the action. What had happened long ago was done anew. All were thrilled as though caught up in the original event. All felt the ethical power of the rite, which showed the voluntary humiliation of the highest of the race.

The occasion was the celebration of the Washing of the Feet by the Orthodox in the Church of the Holy Sepulchre in Jerusalem in a year that I happened to be present. In fact, every year all the main scenes of the Holy Week story, culminating in the Crucifixion and Resurrection, are enacted there by several ancient Christian churches. No one who has been present could forget the dramatic force of, for example, the Abyssinians piteously searching for the vanished body of the Lord before Easter morning, or the Greek Orthodox spreading by candles the light of the Resurrection from the mysterious flame in the Holy Sepulchre.

These strongly traditional churches only preserve amply what is present in some degree in most Christian worship. Wherever there is a 'church calendar', holy days or seasons, there is commemoration and re-enactment. Wherever the Eucharist or Last Supper is celebrated, there is actualization, experience of the original event through drama. In the Jewish tradition, the Passover is an obvious case of worship taking the form of re-enacting the sacred story. A meal is eaten in the manner in which the forefathers were said to have eaten at the Exodus, and the worshippers enter into the Exodus experience; they act out a drama and become one with the first generation. Their own identities are not laid aside in character-acting, but rather taken up into an ideal relationship.

In the ancient Near East sacred drama can be traced back to very early times. A document from Egypt, for example the Ramasseum Dramatic Papyrus, may descend from the beginnings of the Egyptian kingdom. It contains forty-six scenes of a drama, each with description and interpretation of the action, conversation of the gods, and stage directions, and there are thirty-one drawings in illustration. This drama concerns the maintenance of divine order through the accession of a new king, and so was intimately connected with a major theme of Egyptian festivals. In Mesopotamia chief annual festivals are known where the central action was the re-enacting of the battle that established the world and its order and the annual destinies; a subsidiary action signified the renewal of the human king's appointment to serve the heavenly kingship. Public fasting and feasting and assistance at processions made all the population participants in the re-enactments.

In considering the main elements of Israelite drama reflected in the Psalms, we shall concentrate on two areas. The first, which I shall call the 'drama of revelation', exhibits the central event of Israelite worship and shows the chief festival itself as, in a sense, a drama in which all the worshippers had a part to play – again, not putting off their own identity, but raising it to the ideal. The second, which I shall call the 'drama of the Representative', sets forth the vocation of the house of David, without losing the participation of all the worshippers.

1. The drama of revelation
The hardest thing about religion is the hiddenness of God. Human beings, who make their way in life by seeing and

hearing and touching, must reckon here with the reality inaccessible to these senses. Into this situation comes the Old Testament with its chief message: the utterly mysterious one, who has produced all that our senses know, and yet himself eludes them, he has willed to reveal himself in particular circumstances and in a very rich way, entering into bonds of fellowship. Well known, of course, are the Old Testament stories of great patriarchs and prophets receiving such revelation; well known, too, the tradition that at Mount Sinai he confirmed a 'covenant' or bond with the people 'Israel'. But from modern study of the Psalms now appears something more – how year by year in the chief festivals the chief experience was of God's self-revelation. The pilgrims believed that when they assembled in the time, manner and place which he had appointed, he, the hidden reality, would break through to them. And so, many of the Psalms refer to his coming among them with power, and they express the awe and jubilation with which the great assembly reacts. Usually it is the festal season in the autumn which we should think of, the antecedents of the present Jewish New Year's Day, Day of Atonement, and Week of Tabernacles; narratives in the Old Testament show that this was generally the chief pilgrimage festival of the year.

The revealed Lord speaks
To trace the dramatic flow of this season in due order from beginning to end would involve us in many complications. It may be best, therefore, to begin in the middle of the action with something well attested in the Psalms: the speeches of the God who has come in power. And what could be more eloquent of revelation in the midst of the festival than this opening of Psalm 50?

> The Lord, God of gods,
> speaks and summons the world
> from the rising of the sun to its setting.
> Out from Zion, perfection of beauty,
> God shines.

118

Our God has come and is not silent,
fire consumes before him
and tempest rages about him,
he summons the heavens above
and the earth to the judgement of his people.

The singer here is like a prophet, for beyond the framework of
the festal ceremonies – the processions, offerings, incense,
trumpet signals etc. – he apprehends the divine presence with
visionary faculty and expresses it in inspired poetry. But
especially what follows shows his prophetic faculty, for he
claims to mediate words for God in direct speech:

Gather my covenanters before me,
those who share in my covenant through meal of sacrifice!
(50.5)

Soon we hear the singer represent God's voice in a long
and poetic speech to the congregation, full of wit and irony.
It is clear from this that, with all the ritual setting of
mystery and emotion, there was a tradition of deep ethical
reasoning and social criticism. Here is a part of God's
speech:

What do I care if you recite my statutes
and take my covenant upon your mouth
but in practice you reject discipline
and you toss my commands behind your back?
If you see a thief you abet him
and you have a part with adulterers!
You stretch your mouth to evil
and your tongue you yoke with falsehood,
sitting with others you malign your brother,
on your own mother's son hang a calumny!
(50.16–20)

A similar dramatic moment, with revelation and speech, is
embodied in another great text, Psalm 81. Here the manifes-

tation of the deity is marked, not with description as in our previous example, but with calls to acclaim it with chanted cries, and strings, drums and horns:

> Shout acclaim to God our glory,
> shout cries of triumph for the God of Jacob,
> make music and sound the drums,
> sweet lyres and harps together!
> Blow the horns as for new moon,
> as for full moon on the day of our festival!
>
> (81.1–3)

The symphony of greeting dies away, and the inspired singer gives expression to the divine voice, again in direct speech and in fine poetry. God refers to the salvation of the Exodus and to his basic commandments. He promises care and provision, but demands loyalty and integrity. The tone is sombre, in view of human deviousness:

> Hear my people as I admonish you!
> Israel, if only you would listen to me!
>
> (81.8)

The Lord as triumphant King

Of the same structure as Psalm 81 is Psalm 95, again acclaiming the self-revelation of God and then conveying his stern speech. Here the speech exhorts the congregation not to harden their hearts against the divine guidance, as did the fathers in the wilderness. The divine voice ominously points out that that generation made God sick, till he swore none of them should enter the promised land. Again the festal rejoicing is balanced by a tradition of social criticism. The possibility of the rejection and doom of all present is clearly implied. The opening acclaim in this psalm is notable in picturing God's self-revelation as the triumph of his *kingship*, meaning his role as Creator, life-giver, and supreme power over all in heaven and earth.

120

Come, let us shout acclaim to the Lord,
let us give the triumph-cries for the rock that saves us!
Let us acclaim him with music and chant,
for the Lord is supreme God,
truly the great King above all the gods!
To him belong the remotest parts of the earth
and the peaks of the mountains also.
He owns the sea, having made it himself,
he owns the dry land, for his hands moulded it.

(95.1–5)

Now this kingship of God is proclaimed in a number of psalms
– not taught as in sermons or lectures that may lull to sleep,
but proclaimed in dramatic freshness, to be greeted with an
explosion of cheering, clapping, dancing and jubilant music.
It is obvious that the cry 'The Lord is King!' means that
something had happened. It is tremendous news. The moment
has been reached in the drama of the festival where the defeat of
evil has been symbolized and the triumph of the Creator enacted.
It is like the dawn of a new era, a new reign of salvation:

The Lord is now King!
Vested in majesty
vested is the Lord,
girded with glory!
Now the world is secured,
it will not rock. . .

(93.1)

Sing to the Lord a new song,
sing to the Lord all the world,
sing to the Lord, bless his name,
take the news of his victory from day to day,
tell his glory among the nations,
his marvellous deeds among all peoples. . .
dance because of him, all the earth,
say among the nations, The Lord is now King!
Now the world is secured and will not rock,
he rules the peoples with justice.

121

Let heaven make merry and earth rejoice,
thunder the sea and all that lives in it,
let fields exult and all that is in them,
trees sing out, all trees of the forest,
before the Lord, for he has entered,
he has come to rule the earth. . .

(96.1f.)

What a lot of experience and faith and hope are condensed in
this scene of God as manifest King! Here is something of the
turn to life in the seasons, something of the great deliverances
of nations and individuals, something of the belief in the
creation – creation for a good purpose – and something of the
faith that good will triumph and at the last 'all manner of
things shall be well'. And all not as teaching, or sermon, or
poetry recital, but as drama into which all the worshippers are
plunged. To them it was a decisive and creative experience.
God revealed himself in glory and the world was new. We
might say it was a sacrament which replenished all the springs
of faith and hope and moral resolve.

The conquest of chaos

The drama can be traced back a scene, since the psalms which
thus depict God as revealed and acknowledged King sometimes allude to a preceding battle in which he has triumphed.
The adversary may take the form of mighty waters, as in two
splendid psalms of archaic style and concentrated power, 93
and 29. After proclaiming the kingship of the Lord, his robing
in royal splendour, and the stability of his realm, the singer of
Psalm 93 describes the preceding triumph:

Lifted the rivers, Lord,
then lifted the rivers their thunder,
lifted the rivers their splendour.
Over the tumult of their lordships the Waters,
over their majesties the Breakers of the Sea
prevailed in majesty on high the Lord!

(93.3–4)

122

Psalm 29 is also from a scene of God's self-revelation as king. He has taken his throne above the heavenly ocean and the cry goes up for all in heaven and on earth to prostrate themselves and together chant 'Glory!'. But again reference is made to the tremendous acts of power which preceded his ascension. He spoke with claps of thunder to quell the water-foes, causing trepidation in the loftiest mountains and giant trees:

> The Lord's thunder-voice struck the Waters,
> the glorious God thundered,
> the Lord against their lordships the Waters,
> the voice of the Lord went with might,
> the voice of the Lord forth with majesty,
> the voice of the Lord breaking cedars,
> then the Lord shattered the cedars of Lebanon,
> then made he Mount Lebanon skip like a calf
> and Mount Hermon like a young wild-ox,
> the voice of the Lord cleaving flames of fire,
> the voice of the Lord set the wilderness whirling,
> set whirling the wilderness of Kadesh,
> the voice of the Lord sent writhing great oaks
> and stripped bare the forests.
> Now in his palace all say 'Glory!'
> The Lord has taken his throne on the ocean,
> the Lord thrones as King for ever,
> the Lord will give life to his people,
> the Lord will bless his people with prosperity!
>
> (29.3–11)

Such victory over the waters is rich in symbolism. By dynamic struggle the Creator subdues chaos, which is whatever opposes good life and rises arrogantly against the rule of good – it is evil, destruction and death. But he makes the waters then to serve his purpose of life. From them he will give growth and gifts of life. So it was in the beginning, when he cleft the water-power with a mighty blow and drove the water-sources to their places of service in his created order (74. 12–17; 104.6–13). So it is in the present, when all hangs upon his supremacy over chaos. And so it shall be when the age-long drama is resolved and death is for ever swallowed up in victory. Such were the tones of meaning with which, through such psalms, the autumn festival reverberated.

Processions as dramatic action

There is another kind of psalm which helps us to see how the Lord's battle with the waters was represented in the festal ceremonies. These are psalms projecting a triumphal procession, especially 24 and 68. It is fairly clear that the procession depicted here was part of the dramatic enactment of God's conquest of chaos. Processions in Babylonia and Assyria had a similar significance, divine symbols being taken in warlike procession from the temple to a shrine outside the city, where the subjection of the sea was signified before the procession returned in triumph.

For Psalm 68 the Lord himself is returning to his temple victorious. The opening words resemble the verse used when the ark, symbol of God's presence, was lifted for a journey (Num.10.35), and it is likely that it was carried in the procession to indicate his participation. Sacrifices may have been made at the outset, as in David's ceremony (2 Sam.6.13), and images and wax effigies destroyed in flames:

> Let God arise and his enemies be scattered
> and his foes flee before him!
> Like driving of smoke, so drive them away,
> like melting of wax at the fire,
> so perish the wicked at the presence of God!
> But let the righteous make merry,
> exult before God and rejoice with glad noise!
> Sing to God, sing and play to his name,
> prepare the way for him who rides the clouds,
> with (chanting of) his name 'Yah' exult before him!...
> They see your procession, O God,
> the procession of my God and my King into the sanctuary.
> First go the singers, at the rear the harpers,
> surrounded by girls playing hand-drums.
>
> (68.1–4, 24–5)

124

Note 'they *see* your procession, O God'. The onlookers participate; they see the revelation and know the power that not only conquers chaos, but also relieves the sorrowful and renews life:

> As father of the fatherless,
> judge that helps the widows,
> God enters his holy residence,
> God who resettles the lonely in families
> and leads out the prisoners in jubilation. . .
> Rich winter rains you will shake out, O God,
> your land so weary you will make fertile!
>
> (68.5–6,9)

The revelation was spread to ever-widening circles by running of messengers before and around the procession; these seem to be prophetic groups, and apparently women, singing and dancing to express the gospel that the Lord comes in triumph and salvation:

> The Lord gives the word,
> the women bearing tidings are a great host!
>
> (68.11)

A reference to doves may indicate that these were released at the outlying station to fly back to Zion in signal of salvation; the flash of a bird's wing in the bright sunlight is caught thus:

> See, the dove's wings covered with silver,
> her plumage gleaming with gold!
>
> (68.13)

In so small a thing, much is revealed. The whole ceremony, of course, was small for its mighty theme, and the processional way and the temple hill were small for the truths they signified. To the worshippers the ceremonies showed the triumph of God above the heavens, and in this spirit the psalm ends:

125

All sovereignties of the world, sing to God,
sing and play to the Lord!
He who rides on the ancient heaven of heavens,
he it was who uttered his voice, his mighty thunder.
Acknowledge that all might belongs to God!
Over Israel see his splendour
and his glory in the clouds!
You are revealed in dread might, O God,
from out of your sanctuary!
The God of Israel, he it is
who gives vitality and strength to the people.
Blessed be God!

(68.32–5)

From that extended and picturesque treatment of the procession, we turn to a fine compact psalm which concentrates on the moment of entry through the temple gates, Psalm 24. One should catch a triumphant tone in the opening statement, which reflects the preceding subjugation of the water-powers by the Lord:

The Lord is master of the earth and all that fills it,
his is the world and all that live in it,
for it is he who has founded it on the seas,
yes, on top of the rivers he has fixed it!

(24.1–2)

As earlier, we find exacting standards declared in the midst of the festal revelation. The ascent to the temple gates gives rise to searching thoughts, expressed in a dialogue of question and answer:

Who may ascend the mountain of the Lord,
who may stand in his holy temple?

(24.3)

The answer is given in ethical terms, which probably also imply shunning false gods:

126

One clean of palms and pure of heart,
who has not lifted his soul to vanity
nor pledged himself to falsehood –
such shall carry home blessing from the Lord's presence
and happiness from God his saviour.

(24.4–5)

Soon the singer is addressing the gates, which represent the eternal gates of heaven; they are to admit not just a human procession, but the triumphant Creator-king:

O gates, lift up your heads,
be lifted up, eternal doors,
that the all-glorious King may enter!

(24.7)

As though from the gate-keepers, we hear the response:

Who then is the all-glorious King?

(24.8)

This is answered with reference to the victory:

The Lord, the mighty one and champion,
the Lord, champion in war!
O gates, lift up your heads,
be lifted up, eternal doors,
that the all-glorious King may enter!

(24.8–9)

And again the challenge:

But who then is the all-glorious King?

(24.10)

And so the final response, citing the name before which all must give way:

The Lord of Hosts (Yahweh Sebaoth),
he is the all-glorious King!

(24.10)

Taking part in the drama

We have now sampled the more obvious psalms that helped to
convey the festal revelation. Many more psalms may be
connected with this event in worship, and it seems that the
whole collection reverberates with it. Appropriately, at the
end of the collection, Psalm 150 discloses the festal scene with
unmatched economy and ecstasy. The contributions of music
and dancing and drama flow into one in this tremendous
scene. The excitement is the measure of the event: the
revelation of the Creator. Before the manifest Lord the temple
musicians are giving of their best and loudest, with horns,
lyres, harps, drums, pipes, and the cymbals that proclaim
victory. Dancers whirl, and the final cry goes out:

Every breathing thing, praise the Lord!

All our study of the arts in the Psalms has brought out the
fundamental theme of the praise of the Creator. Yet the virtue
of such intense and extended praising may not be self-evident.
For whose benefit is it, for whose pleasure? Would we wish
such praise from our own subordinates? Our present study
helps us here, for it shows the call to praise as a call to
participate in the drama of revelation. Those who join in the
festal praises are committing themselves in the events of the
drama; they are playing a part in the symbolic coming of God's
kingdom, siding with the Creator in his contest with evil. The
poetry that portrays him and his work of power and love, the
poetry of praise, is a sacrament of words. To receive it with
cries of assent and choruses is to see the face of the Lord and
feel his powerful presence. The architecture has provided the
ideal stage, a bridge between heaven and earth. The music
breathes divine life into the poetry, which now wings its way
into heaven as easily as into the human heart. The dancing
leads to a total commitment, when body and spirit, individual

and community, are wholly given to God's cause. As the worshippers join in the drama of praise with lifting of voices, bending of bodies and dancing of feet, they orient themselves to reality, acknowledging the greatness which is not themselves, and so find new life.

The drama uses elements of mythology: the Creator fights and ascends and reigns from his house. But this is only to say that great issues and problems of existence have been turned into the language of story. How potent is story, how universal its appeal! But still more so, when turned into a drama in which all present take a part! Through this means the little temple of a little state could involve the simple population in issues of cosmic proportions – the origin of the world, its present meaning, its final end, the significance of mankind, the relation of all species; such mighty questions were grasped and clarified in the lines of a story, the story of the Creator's work of salvation. The festival turned it into a drama, a doing-as-for-the-first-time. It plucked the story from all the ages, plunged the worshippers into it, bathed them in the revelation of reality, and so gave purification, hope, and resolve.

2. The drama of the Representative

Supporting the central drama of the festival as just described were other themes which were also treated in dramatic ceremonies. In the preparation of the people there were rites of atonement, such as that of the scapegoat when an animal, symbolically loaded with the people's guilt, was driven out into the wilderness (Lev.16). The sanctuary would likewise be cleansed and prepared for the time when, with the new entry of the Lord, it could be said that holiness again adorned the house (Ps.93.5). The city of Jerusalem was strengthened again in the promises of God's protection by a dramatic enactment of his fidelity to that promise:

> We have enacted your fidelity, O God,
> in the centre of your temple.

(48.9)

129

Kings were shown to flee, ships to be broken up, when God appeared as Zion's defender (48.3–8). Worshippers making procession around the walls took the part of the beleaguered who could now go out to survey the miraculously preserved city (48.12–14).

The festal setting

Not the least among these supporting themes was that of the renewal of the king's office and grace. Since the festival was all about God's reign, it was natural to include in its themes the calling of the chief agent of that reign, the king of David's line, the Lord's anointed. A comparable practice is known in neighbouring countries, such as Egypt and Mesopotamia, where also, amidst the festal celebration of the divine order or kingship, the consecration of its earthly agent was renewed. Such festivals were the setting for the first full enthronement of a new king, while forms of renewal took place in subsequent years.

The goal of the drama

Such is the likely context for a number of colourful psalms which treat of the royal office. Idealistic, archetypal, visionary, psalms such as 2 and 110 were in much later times simply used as prophecies of the Messiah of the last days. But another quality too stands out. They are dramatic. Speaker yields to speaker. Mighty events take place in symbol. Arranged together, they easily form a 'plot'. In their original usage, therefore, they were surely linked with rites that dramatically set forth the king's office as chief servant of the heavenly King. We should probably think of a self-contained ritual sequence concerning the human king's position, carried out separately from the drama of God's own triumph. Perhaps, as in Mesopotamia, it served to prepare him to take his part in the greater celebration. The effect was to show how the Lord had provided an earthly representative to carry out his will, and how he would give him all triumph if he kept to the path of humility and faith. Culminating scenes appear in Psalm 21:

130

Lord, in your power the king rejoices
and in your salvation how greatly he delights!
The desire of his heart you have given him
and the request of his lips you have not refused,
Truly you have met him with blessings of good,
you have placed on his head a crown of fine gold.
Life he asked of you and you have given it him,
length of days for ever and ever.
Great is his glory in your salvation,
you have placed on him splendour and majesty. . .

(21.1–15)

With this establishment of a king in God's favour, set to carry
out God's will, there was prospect of good conditions in
society and nature:

O God, give your judgments to the king
and your right order to the royal one,
may he judge your people with righteousness
and your humble ones with justice!
The mountains shall then bear prosperity for the people
and the hills (rejoice) in the bounty of right order.

(72.1–3)

Encounter with evil foes
But this peaceful prospect was not reached without due
treatment of the theme of evil. Much was said and no doubt
done in the rites to signify God's gift of triumph over the
chaotic forces on earth. Hence Psalm 110, where a message
from God is delivered to the king:

Sit at my right hand
while I make your enemies
a footstool for your feet. . .
The Lord upon your right hand
crushes kings on the day of his anger,
he executes judgment on the nations,
makes many corpses,
smites through heads across the wide earth.

(110.1,5–6)

Just how imaginative the drama was can be seen from Psalm 2. The king confronts a world of hostility against the reign of the Lord and his anointed king:

> Why do the nations make uproar
> and the peoples seethe with mischief?
> Why do earth's kings stand up
> and the rulers hold conclave
> against the Lord and his anointed
> (saying) 'Let us break their bonds,
> throw off from us their cords'?
> He who thrones in heaven laughs,
> the Lord of all derides them,
> speaks then to them in his anger
> and in his wrath confounds them (saying)
> 'Enough that I have anointed my king
> on Zion my holy mountain!'

(2.1–6)

The world's order is thus made to hinge on the installation of the king. He continues his address with an informative reference to the ceremony in question – how he was given a document of promise from the Lord:

> I will quote the Lord's document;
> he says to me:
> 'You are now my son,
> I this day have become your father.
> You have only to ask
> and I will give you the nations as your heritage
> and the ends of the earth as your property!'

(2.7–8)

A ceremony of shattering symbolic jars may be reflected as he continues quoting from the document:

> 'With a sceptre of iron
> you will break them
> and smash them

like potter's jars!'
Now then, you kings, be prudent,
back to discipline, rulers of the earth!

(2.9–10)

A time of trial

So far, then, we have trodden fairly firm ground along the
path of exploration into this ritual sequence. It is clear that in
dramatic fashion the rites showed how God chose a king who,
if obedient, would serve God's purpose in victory over evil.
We can take another important step without much danger.
From Psalm 101 it is plain that the drama showed how
important it was for the king to rule according to God's will. If
imagination and symbol were needed to hammer home the
defeat of chaos, no less were they valuable to enforce the
lesson of the king's dependence on the Lord. It is not
surprising, then, that in Psalm 101, when the king has to
promise to act justly, his situation seems to be dramatized as
one of trial and need for God. He speaks as from a situation of
peril and God-forsakenness. In the pathetic lamenting style he
pleads that God will soon come to save him:

Of loyalty and justice I would sing,
to you, Lord, raise a psalm,
my theme the way of integrity, –
Oh when will you come to me?
I will walk with a true heart within my house,
I will not contemplate the planning of evil.
Corrupt practices I abhor,
  they shall not stick to me.
I shall dismiss the man of crooked heart
  and have no share with the wicked.
One who puts the evil word on his neighbour
  I will put to death.
The arrogant and high-handed
  I will not endure.
I will look for the most faithful in the earth
  to consort with me.

133

He who walks the way of integrity
   is the one to serve me.
In all my palace there shall not dwell
   a dealer in deceit.
The speaker of falsehood shall not endure
   the gaze of my eyes.
Daily at sunrise I will sentence
   all the wicked of the earth,
to cut off from the city of the Lord
   all dealers in iniquity.

                                         (101.1–8)

The poetry here uses the metre favoured for laments, and the whole point of the avowal is given in the pathetic question, 'Oh when will you come to me?' Now it happens that a scene is known in the great festival of Babylon where the king has to make avowal of a just reign in obedience to his god, and he has to make it in a pathetic situation. Before the god's presence in the temple of Babylon the king approaches and is stripped of his regalia by the chief priest, who also strikes his cheek and drags him by the ears before the god's symbol and makes him bow to the ground. In this position the king must say:

I did not sin, lord of the countries,
I was not neglectful of the requirement of your
godship...
I did not rain blows on the cheek of a subordinate...
I did not humiliate them,
I watched out for Babylon, I did not smash its walls...

Eventually the priest expresses the god's favourable response: he will hear his prayer, destroy his foes and bless him for ever. So the king receives back his regalia, but with them another reminder of dependence, for the re-invested king is given another blow, and his tears must flow if the promise of victory is to be confirmed. It is only after this ceremonial that the Babylonian king then takes his part in the festival.

   Such a comparison with a leading Semitic people of the period does not of course prove anything for Israel, but it should give us more insight to interpret the biblical data.

Out of the depths

Now among the Psalms there are several which depict the Davidic king as almost swallowed up by chaos or death, but delivered by God from the very depths. Most commentators suggest that the reference is to deliverance in historical battles, portrayed picturesquely. But when due consideration is given to all the material, with the less disputed festal texts that we have just studied, the view advocated chiefly by A.R. Johnson may be preferred, namely, that these colourful depictions of salvation from chaos come also from dramatic festal scenes. We would have a splendid example in Psalm 118. Here is a joyful festal procession; through the temple gates is led the victorious figure, – surely the king. He tells of a scene where a world of hostility had surrounded him:

> All nations surrounded me...
> surrounded me like bees –
> by the name of the Lord I cut them down!
> The Lord chastised me severely
> but did not give me over to death...
> The stone which the builders rejected
> has become the head of the corner-tower[1]

(118.10f.)

The procession passes into the main court and, with dancing step, circles round the great altar.

Another psalm looking back on such a scene of peril is Psalm 18. Here the king's encounter with chaos is vividly portrayed as a sinking into the watery jaws of the underworld, deep in the oceans. As promised, however, the Lord heard his prayer and, in proof that the supplicant was faithful, had rescued him – but what a rescue!

> In his temple he heard my voice
> and my cries entered his ears.
> Then quaked the earth and trembled,
> the mountain bases rocked,
> they quaked, for his anger blazed,

135

his nostrils smoked,
fire blazed from his mouth,
from him came fiery coals.
The heavens he bent and descended,
black cloud beneath his feet.
He mounted his cherub-steed and flew,
swooped on wings of wind...
The Lord thundered from heaven,
the Most High uttered his voice
with hail and fiery coals.
Yes, he shot his arrows and scattered them,
shot lightning in plenty and confused them.
Exposed were the channels of the ocean,
the dry land's bases laid bare
by your battle-roar, Lord,
by the blast of your nostrils!
So he reached from on high and took me up,
drew me up from the great waters...

(18.6f.)

Now as one ponders the likelihood that this refers to a ritual scene, one may compare Psalm 144, with several similar lines, which would fit as the cry for help before the deliverance:

Lord, what is man that you should heed him,
a mere man that you should think of him,
man fleeting as a puff of air,
his days passing as a shadow?
Lord, bend your heavens and descend,
touch the mountains in fire and smoke,
shoot lightnings and scatter them,
shoot your arrows and confuse them,
reach with your hand from on high,
save and deliver me front the great waters,
    from the alien powers...

(144.3f.)

It is very significant that this prayer of the king ends with indication of what the deliverance will mean for society; it will mean healthy order in nature, with healthy birth, growth and provision:

> Save and deliver me. . .
> so that our sons may be like plants
>   well-grown when still young,
> our daughters columns
>   carved for the building of a palace,
> our barns full of all provisions,
> our flocks increasing by thousands and ten thousands
>   in our fields
> our cattle heavy with young,
> bearing without mishap in due time,
> and no cry of pain in our courts. . .
>
> (144.11f.)

Surely there is more involved here than the outcome of a battle. The sequence of thought points rather to the rites where the foundations of life were explored, and the king's relation to God was shown as fundamental to the life of all society. If the Lord found him worthy, he would channel blessings of life through him into the world.

Another major text calls for consideration, the mighty Psalm 89. Here the king reviews in measured and ample fashion his work as witness to the Lord's fidelity, and gives a beautiful exposition of God's covenant with the founder of the dynasty, David. At last he turns to his lament, making a pointed contrast with the promises just expounded. Here he is, the heir of these promises, in a pitiable condition, as though rejected and despised by this same covenant Lord. His lot is defeat. His crown and throne are flung to the ground. His days of youthful strength are cut short, the Lord has wrapped him in shame. This psalm will not fit directly any historical situation, and its grand, expansive manner might better suit the great rites.

Taking stock
So far, then, our quest for the 'drama of the Representative'

137

has found some firm ground from which further exploration could be made. It appeared that the enthronement of the Davidic kings and the annual renewals of the office were accomplished in dramatic ceremonies. Elevation to the high office of God's steward was carried out in successive scenes that showed how all power and victory were of God, and were only for the man chosen by him, steadfast in faith and humility, committed to the battle with evil. Through such a representative, God would effect blessings for all society. I then raised the question as to how far the drama showed the anointed as humiliated before being finally exalted. Psalm 101 (with the Babylonian comparison) and Psalm 144 seemed to give a firm lead here, and more detail and colour could be added in the light of A.R. Johnson's exposition of Psalms 118, 18 and 89, although most commentators still look for non-ritual explanations.

The drama of the royal calling, on the view proposed, was a most significant interpretation of life. It showed a man chosen by the deity to represent his cause on earth. And this chosen one is also the representative of men, as he works to secure the life and blessing of all society. The way he takes is a model for all. For the sake of the right and the true, he must expose himself to chaotic horrors. Victory springs out of his darkest hour, when his allegiance to the divine reality is tried to the uttermost. If the victory seems to be expressed sometimes in too lurid, martial terms, one must remember that there the power of poetry is used to battle with seemingly omnipotent evil and assert its conquest by the truth. A world's happiness is found to be built on that one point of utter helplessness where one frail human being was almost overwhelmed with the weight of evil and death; but because he still held to the truth, that helplessness turned out to be the point where the conquering power of God could pour into the world.

The performance of the drama appears to have used means not unlike those still found in worship and in royal ceremony today: chanted speeches pass from one party to another, processions and entries through gates signify progress in the action, prostration means humiliation, ascension means glory,

138

lack of robes and insignia contrasts with investiture and bestowal of sceptre and crown, authority is conveyed in the gift of scroll or title-deeds, grace and holiness are imparted with washing and anointing and sacred drink. As in Egypt, destruction of inscribed pots might indicate victory over foes. The great range of dramatic symbolism enacted by the Israelite prophets and recounted in the prophetic and histori- cal books (Isa.20; Jer.19; Ezek.4–5 etc.) will be related to the festal action. Like these prophetic mimes, the festal drama uses symbolism and imitative acting to set forth a work of God.

Other dramatic psalms of death and life
Are there other important psalms which may have formed part of the royal rites, the drama of the Representative, though rarely seen in this light today? It is worth looking at two of the best-known psalms from this point of view, Psalms 22 and 23. Psalm 22 lends itself to such a dramatic interpretation, since it consists of two contrasting scenes which can scarcely be explained on any other view. It also has an archetypal character, pressing its images to the ultimate, and it contains royal themes. Psalm 23 can be added to the consideration because it sets a seal on the dramatic movement of Psalm 22 in a way which justifies its position as the following psalm. No claim can be made for the certainty of the following exposi- tion. But the reader may judge how far the texts lend themselves to the proposed setting in drama, matching the role they were to play in a later age in the drama of the Christian liturgy.

Psalm 22 divides into two opposing scenes: verses 1–21 are a lament from the sphere of death, verses 22–31 a celebration in the place of life. How bitingly the first begins! – for the phrase 'my God' alludes to a bond with God and his promises of care:

My God, my God, why have you forsaken me,
staying far from my crying,
from my shouts for help?
My God, I called to you all day

139

> – and you have not answered,
> all night (I cried) without ceasing.
> There are you, seated in holy majesty,
> celebrated God of Israel,
> in whom our fathers trusted,
> trusted and you delivered them;
> to you they cried and were rescued,
> in you they trusted and were vindicated.
> And here am I, worm rather than man,
> mockery of mankind, butt of all people.
>
> (22.1–6)

The mockery centres on the fact that here is one specially chosen by God and treated as his son – here is such a one unprotected, God-forsaken!

> All who gloat over me mock me
> with pouting lips and wagging heads,
> 'So this is the Lord's man!
> Let him deliver him,
> let him save him,
> this man of his favour!'
> Yes, you were the one to draw me from the womb,
> and to lay me on the breasts of my mother,
> on to you was I cast out from the womb,
> from my mother's belly you have been my God.
> Do not stay far from me, now that anguish is come
> and I have no helper!
>
> (22.7–11)

So far the appeal has centred on the special bond of the sufferer with God, the pathos that this most beloved one should now be left alone in his torment. Now the appeal develops by depicting the anguish movingly. The lonely figure is beset by death; the horrors of decay and dissolution swim over him, naked and drained of strength; the animals of hell encircle him greedily, gaping and baying and biting:

140

Huge bulls encircle me,
fat bulls of Bashan surround me,
they open wide their mouths over me,
lions that rend and roar.
I am all drained out like water,
all my bones come apart,
my heart has become like wax
melted inside my bowels,
my life-force is dried up like a sherd,
my tongue sticks to my jaws,
yes, you have put me in the pit of death,
and death's dogs surround me,
the pack of cruel demons encircle me,
tearing at my hands and feet.
I can count all my bones
as the mockers gloat over me.
They have shared out my clothes as spoil,
for my clothing they have thrown lots.

(22.12–18)

This is the nakedness of death; the demons share out the clothes like spoil of war. Surely this is the end for him? Yet the appeal has been made and comes to rest thus:

But you, Lord, do not stand aloof!
My only help, speed to my aid!
Deliver my life from the sword,
my dear soul from the grip of the dog!
Save me from the mouth of the lion,
from the horns of the wild bulls,
you must answer me!

(22.19–21)

The scene now changes. The appeal has been answered and all is celebration. Could this be the turning point in the whole 'drama of the Representative'? In the midst of the festal congregation the man of God's favour, proved and triumphant, blesses the distribution of the thanksgiving

141

sacrifices, a joyful meal of communion, and he sees the salvation of God as echoing to the bounds of space and time. This is how he concludes his thanksgiving:

> Let all the earth's bounds celebrate this
> and return to the Lord,
> and all families of the nations
> worship before you!
> Yes, to the Lord belongs the kingship
> and he is the ruler over the nations!
> The living on earth eat together as they worship,
> those gone down to the underworld bow before him,
> for he has made my soul live again to him!
> My descendants shall serve him,
> testimony shall be made to the Lord
> by my generations.
> They too shall make solemn entry
> and announce his righteous work,
> to a people yet to be born (they shall say)
> 'He has done it!'

(22.27–31)

He has done it, he has acted; the drama is done. It has been shown that from the point where the man of God's favour, one like a son to him, was exposed to all death's torments, from that one point grows a great kingdom of life. The call goes out to all earth's families to acknowledge the Lord the King. Even the underworld reverberates with the impact of the salvation. Generations yet unborn will receive the testimony and share this new life of praise.

A serene interlude

After the exciting testimony from the second scene of Psalm 22, Psalm 23 sounds like further testimony in a third scene of serenity and repose. The singer portrays himself alone with the Lord, who acts for him as shepherd and host. Enemies there are, but kept at bay by the mighty protector, and given notice by the ceremony of a meal that this protection is

142

enduring. The signs are that it is the Representative who sings this testimony, the royal figure. But what lies behind his serene testimony, his confidence of being the protégé of the Lord who, as Shepherd-king, is stronger than the grim shepherd Death? Most appropriate would be the deliverance enacted in the preceding psalm, a deliverance, I have suggested, in symbol and drama. After such a demonstration of the Lord's rescue of his chosen one from the very jaws of death, the king would now look to his future destiny with confidence.

The beautiful imagery would echo the symbolism of the preceding rites, the Lord's role as shepherd with rod and staff expressing his kingship with sceptre and crozier. The pastures and streams then represent the very gift of life; the leading on the road of righteousness or salvation reflects the triumphal procession; and the honour of God's name is the theme of his having stood by the covenant with his chosen one:

> With the Lord as my shepherd, I want for nothing.
> In green pastures he will give me rest,
> by peaceful waters he will lead me,
> he will restore my soul.
> He will conduct me on roads of salvation
> to the honour of his name.

(23.1–3)

And now a reference to the valley of the shadow of death will reflect that symbolic exposure to the powers of chaos and death:

> Even when I go through the chasm of Death's dominion
> I will fear no evil,
> for you will be with me,
> your royal rod and crook
> will comfort me.

(23.4)

Next, God's laying of a table and his acts of anointing and giving a cup may reflect ceremonies which publicly declared God's choice and promised care of his Representative:

You lay a table before me, a sign to all my foes.
You have anointed my head with oil,
my cup is full.

(23.5)

Then the promised care is seen as embodied in the angelic beings that attend the king in all his dangerous missions. His hope to return to God's house reflects the royal vocation to sit at God's right hand (cf.110.1):

Truly Grace and Fidelity will closely attend me
all the days of my life,
and I shall return to the house of the Lord
for years without number.

(23.6)

This most beloved of all psalms, placed in this context, is no facile assertion of God's kindliness. The underlying rite would have presented the deepest truth that could ever be known to poet, prophet, dramatist or musician. It was a climactic event drawn from all that had ever happened and all that would ever happen. In the drama of the Representative encountering death, it spoke of the partnership of God and man, of the issues of creation, life, suffering, integrity, death, and hope overcoming death.

The peace of Psalm 23 thus has underlying it an immense depth. To enter this text and share its tender intimacy must be by way of a daunting journey. It would be necessary to find our way, through the circumstances peculiar to ourselves, to that place where the Representative suffers to the uttermost and holds true and obtains victory; and somehow we should have to stand with him in the darkness, and only then could we return with him to the house of the Lord for ever.

7

PUTTING IT ALL TOGETHER

The Word and the arts
'In the beginning was the Word.' Shall we then, of all the ancient arts, give the crown to poetry? In *Vision in Worship*, a book relating prophecy to psalmody, my conclusion seemed to tend this way:

> 'We may say then that worship in Israel was characterized by the word, above all the poetic word; flying on great wings of imagination, it bore thought and feeling from God to man and from man to God, making a true communion of mind and soul. The vision that illumined Israelite worship was primarily grasped and shared through rapturous poetry, however much it was supported by music, dancing, and drama.'

But the present study has taken the arts in turn and noted the special contribution of each and the claim of each to honour and love. Was my former conclusion biased? Writers indeed tend to claim superiority for the particular art in which they are absorbed. Some speak for dance, as for example Walter Sorell:

> 'Dance is as old as the desire of man to express himself, to set his feeling free, to communicate his joys and sorrows with the most immediate instrument at his disposal: his body ... Movement precedes speech. Rhythm is all-embracing, cosmic.'

Music has often been given peculiar honour, as when Schopenhauer praised it as so much more powerful and impressive than the other arts, since they spoke only of the shadow of reality, but music spoke of reality itself (*Die Welt as Wille und Vorstellung* I.52).

For the art of words, indeed, there may sometimes seem to be a rebuff. In his inspiring book *To a Dancing God*, Sam Keen writes:

> 'There is a time for words. It has lasted from the Reformation to the present. Now we are sick of being inundated in an ocean of verbiage.'

But his real point appears as he continues:

> 'The word must be rediscovered in the flesh. Religion must return to the dance.'

And his book after all contains a fine account of the significance of stories, which in their way spring from the same ground as poetry and drama:

> 'In telling stories, traditional man was affirming the unity of reality... Past, present, and future were ... bound together in a thematic unity... The story affirmed ... the individual ... belonged to a continuity of meaning that the flow of time could not erode... Personality ... is the key to the cosmos. Man is a microcosm; thus in telling stories, he may have confidence that his warm, concrete, dramatic images are not unrelated to the forces that make for the unity of the macrocosm. While his images and stories may reduce the proportions of reality to a scale that is manageable by the human spirit, their distortion serves the cause of truth.'

So it is not a question of disparaging the word, but of rediscovering it in the flesh. The protest is against words used

146

without depth of experience. St John's 'word in the beginning' represents *meaning*, a meaning of grace and truth, life and light, passing through the depths of all created things.

What has to be considered is not which art is chief, but how each contributes to the whole work of holding that meaning before us and drawing our whole selves ever deeper into it. In the end, art is one and its work one; but there are various aspects, which we appreciate the better for having studied them in turn.

Poetry

Our discussion of the poetic art in the Psalms had to move between the Hebrew original and its re-creation in English. Some idea of what was lost in translation and what could live again appeared as I traced the system of Hebrew poetry. We saw how the sentences and clauses flow simply as lines or half-lines. The parts of a line balance rhythmically, and one could count the chief stresses or word-units to give three matching three, three matching two, and many other patterns. Already one felt the power of the words to dance; but with all the force of rhythm, there remained freedom for variety. The power to sing was felt too as we noticed the music of word-sounds. End-rhymes, with their cramping control of rhythm and phrasing, were not a feature of Hebrew poetry. But music ran through the play of consonants and vowels: resonance, lapping sounds, hissings, plosives, the sob or hearty cry from the throat, the pure colours of the vowels.

And as music balances its phrases – repeating exactly, repeating with variation, matching with contrast, now dwelling on a theme, now moving swiftly on, so the poetry proceeded by way of 'parallelism'. Freedom and variety were again obvious as the poets wove beautiful, balancing patterns that again made the statements dance and sing, heightening interest, suspense and emphasis. What cumulative power in the parallel statements which express all the agonies and terrors of the human soul! What ecstasy in the parallel praises of the Creator! And we saw how the method enabled the poet to fill out and develop his theme and present it from various angles, without using intricate structures of sentences.

The simple structure of short clauses favoured economy of wording, and there was no larding with adjectives. The style was lean and close to homely speech. Parallel statements produced favourite pairings of words to match each other, and beyond such pairs little families of related words develop, helping us to feel for their true meaning. Especially important was the family of words expressing the theme of love promised, maintained, and fulfilled – the theme of faithfulness. Here was a great theme to unify past, present and future, and so make us at home in the universe: the promise and commitment lying in our origins, the fulfilment which gladdens our present, the trust which helps us look to the future. This theme is the heart of story, as Sam Keen again explains:

> 'Being the recipient of promises, I become the maker of promises. I seek to manifest that same faithfulness to others which was gratuitously shown to me... I find the principle which gives unity to my life and binds together the past, future and present... I have a story.'

A word we might misunderstand; a statement might then lose its force. But the poetry of the Psalms brings a whole family of words to bear on its theme, and parallel statements support each other to express the message. Thus John Milton, versifying Psalm 136, inherited the misleading translation 'mercy' for *hesed* (which may usually be rendered 'fidelity') but he still grasped the theme well:

> For his mercies aye endure,
> ever faithful, ever sure.

Our review of the poetic imagery of the Psalms brought out their poetic view of the world. Homely images of the cosmic elements and forces did not detract from awe and wonder – quite the contrary. The climate and vegetation of Palestine and its contiguous waters and deserts appear in the poetry, as

148

also do the animals around the home, the beasts of the wild, the fowls of the air, and things that creep. Imagery was drawn too from family life and from work. The mark of it all was simplicity and sincerity.

All the more effective, then, was its most constant application, the finding of God. Here is a God who listens to poetry. He is swayed by poignant imagery when he hears in it the ring of truth. Telling phrases are thus used to express the suppliant's need, his frailty, his persecutions, his horrors, and also his trust. In all the strength of poetry, prayer rises up to confound the enemy, and all his malice, arrogance and falsehood. God the Creator works with craftsman's fingers, God the saviour comes as a warrior. The poetry depicting him is extremely bold, but it brings home his power and love most tellingly. With all his exalted majesty, he is yet concerned with each tiny member of his realm, caring and sustaining. The poet is touched with awe to reflect on the formation of his own body under the hand of God, and the preparation of his days, and the thoughts of God that are more than the sand-grains. To this God, whose glory is told in all the heavens, he can say 'the palm of your hand is upon me', 'keep me like the little one in your eye'.

As regards the form of a psalm as a whole, it appeared that there was at first sight much disparity. When attention was given to the elements of thought making up a psalm, however, progress could be made in defining types of psalm. Such elements of thought had a traditional nature, using traditional words and phrases, and were often combined in fairly regular fashion. The call to praise God and the giving of a reason for the call, for example, yielded the regular pattern of songs of praise scholars call Hymns. The approach to God in great need was voiced in the type of psalm called Laments, where the elements of thought include the plea for a hearing, the moving account of the suffering, the sharp questions, the petition for help, the statement of trust, and sometimes the assurance of having been heard and the vow to give thanks with sacrifice and song. The recognition of such classes of psalm and their functions, a big feature of psalm study in the twentieth

149

century, was a fruitful process if its limitations were kept in mind. The types were not a matter of conscious law, but arose naturally from traditional uses in recurring situations, and would allow development and fluidity as did the situations themselves.

Recognition of form and tradition made all the more fascinating the achievement of freshness and liveliness in this poetry. Here was an interesting example of the interplay of community and individual, custom and originality, genuine feeling expressed through inherited forms. Each needed the other, and they were blended here in especially happy fashion to produce the most eloquent poetry of prayer, praise, and teaching.

The composers and performers of this poetry were most obviously to be found in the families of specialist musicians that served the temple services, a kind of priestly service that did not preclude secular occupations and that could be rendered also by women. Beyond them we could look to the kings, whose role was to be first in prayer and praise before the Lord and to make and sustain the institutions of religion. If one figure were to be picked out as composer and founder, it would best be David – chiming in with tradition.

Architecture

Next we considered the art of fine building. Put to serve a way of life, it comes soon to shape it. Meeting basic physical needs, it ministers also to the whole person, fostering community and communion, furnishing and refreshing the spirit. No less than poetry, it has its forms and proportions, a rhythm of spacing, repetition and grouping; contrasts, balances, and accents. Like poetry too, it responds to nature – to soil and rock, contour and prospect, air, sun and water, heat and cold, flowers and trees.

Architecture for the Psalms centred in Jerusalem, 'foundation of peace', where there was already an important inheritance from earlier peoples. Regard for the travellers' routes, the lie of the mountains and valleys and the flow of a fresh spring guided the development of a compact fortress-city. It was noted how David made it the unifying bond in a great empire, and Solomon gave expression to its importance with extensions and great buildings. For both kings the city's significance was above all that it was the city of God, and it was the home not only of its residents but also of the great assemblies of pilgrim-worshippers, and of all who looked towards it in prayer.

Its processional holy way, leading up the hill and into the temple gates, courts and buildings, spoke of the march of God who fought and triumphed for the salvation of his world; it spoke too of the march of the people of God who, in his steps, had also a way to take, a path to follow for truth and goodness. The glacis and walls of the city spoke of God's protection and the ring of fellowship, ever refreshed by the dew of God's blessing. The gates, as gates of God, were entered with awe and joy. In his courts the worshippers found the centre of their world, the home where they were formed and replenished and prepared for days to come. Here they were open to the sun or to night's starry skies, as they gathered around the great altar, in front of the small, beautiful building that represented the house and throne of the Creator. The architecture here provided both for movement and repose; for the action of the liturgy in procession, prostration, drama, and sacrifice; but also for stillness in the presence of God, peace in the house and home at the centre of all things.

The temple building itself spoke of order, beauty, life, and above all, majesty, the majesty of the Creator. It was a sign that gave contact with the ultimate reality, gave vision of him who reigned above the ocean of heaven. All that could be done to this end by art of siting, proportion, and working of stone, wood, bronze and gold, was done. Steps, pillars and porch, nave and clerestory windows, veil of gold chains, inner sanctum, ark and cherubim overlaid with gold, all spoke of the Presence.

But temple and city were a unity, and the whole too had focal significance. All the life of mankind, of nature and the great elements, was here brought to a focus in relation to the giver of life. From these buildings and enclosed spaces there

was a going out with blessing; and to them again a coming in
to see the meaning afresh.

Music
It was found that the ancient art of music had a great role in
worship and was essential to psalmody. Of the instruments
used in this connection, there was first the lyre, its notes sweet
and lightly resonant. To this was often joined the portable
harp, of fuller, deeper sound. Another eloquence belonged to
the pipes, which could as well moan eerily as spread merri-
ment. Double oboes might provide a droning harmony.

Along with the clapping of hands, there were various
instruments of percussion. These were of great importance,
and no less needed talent and specialist knowledge. The
drums were usually small frame-drums carried by hand or
slung from the shoulder, beaten by hand, the instrument
especially of the young women. In their hands, too, might be
found the 'shakers', which were so full of meaning to the
Egyptians, as though they shook out healing and life from
heaven. The quivering clash of cymbals was no less meaning-
ful, being associated with the gospel of the Lord's coming in
victory. Signals of the approach of the Lord and of holy times
were also given by trumpet and horn, which therefore came
to add their strong and peculiar voices to the orchestra of
praise.

Along with these varied voices sounded the singing: chanting of psalms, concerted acclamations and responses. Skilled
soloists and specialist choirs took the main burden, while the
congregation participated with phrases of assent, supplication,
and praise, and no doubt acts of homage, face to the ground.
Responsive singing, one to the other, suited the fellowship of
worship, just as the calls to praise, so characteristic of Israelite
worship, are also a form of mutual help and encouragement in
the mighty task. The singing was the expression of the strong
feelings of the words, and so took sharply contrasting styles in
accordance with the aim of the words, from tones ringing with
joy to groans and ululations. The inspired cantors and
specialist choirs included women and, as in Egypt, may well

have gathered from various situations and occupations in daily life for periods of service at the temple.

With research progressing into the musical systems of the Babylonians and Canaanites and into the common roots of oriental Jewish and Gregorian chant, and with the accents and rubrics of the Hebrew Bible ever re-examined, the possibility remained of one day reconstructing the musical system of the Hebrews. It appeared, however, that in the meantime we have something perhaps more important: indications of what music *meant* to the people of the Psalms. It was felt as an inspired art, prompted by the spirit of God. With this gift of his grace, offering was made again to him; it was for his delight that the instruments were played and the voices raised. Of all the offerings made in quest of peace and harmony with him, music was most fitted to enter the heavenly realm and find favour.

The music of praise at the great festivals was felt to be an earthly echo or counterpart of the music in heaven. And this scene of musical praise in heaven and on earth before the Lord in his revealed sovereignty was a focus of the continuing relation of Creator and creatures throughout the cosmos. Heaven and sky-vault, day and night, creatures great and small renew their life as they sing to one another in their own manner the songs of the glory of God. With the music of praise the creatures relate themselves to God and commune with him. If God is so known in music, it is not surprising that the art is also a source of enlightenment in life's enigmas. By music the sage would unlock the grievous riddle, by music also convey holy teaching and the light of guidance to his followers. Through intoned recitation, the student of God's law absorbed his words of life and contemplated his will and being with delight.

In the figure of the Lord's anointed was found the chief minstrel of God. This figure, embodying the *ideal* of the king's vocation, is to rule the world on God's behalf, his first servant, and as it were his son. And in his hand the lyre, and in his mouth the song! This is the music of life, which he strikes up for all creation to sing and play with him.

153

Dance

We found that the importance of dancing in the worship of the Psalms was not to be measured by the number of explicit references. With the help of other Old Testament passages and study of such broad terms as 'rejoicing' and 'prophesying', one could see that, from beginning to end of the period, dancing was an essential feature of worship. It was natural for all the feelings present in the approach to God and in the communion with him to find expression in bodily movement. Where these feelings were powerful, as in the festal rejoicing, the movement was correspondingly vigorous. The king himself might take the lead in turning and leaping, even perhaps somersaulting and cartwheeling, 'with all his strength before the Lord'.

The feelings, however, arose in a context of story, as our treatment of drama was to show. The dancing was full of meaning, as when it helped to announce the divine work in the liturgy – the coming of God, his victory, his kingship, and the consequent gospel of salvation.

The dancing of the specialists extended into a bodily rejoicing of all the people. The gospel was spread and the joyful awareness of God and his saving work passed through widening circles. The rhythmic movement to the drums, shakers, strings and pipes was a communion with God, who himself rejoiced at the heart of the fellowship. The world was bathed in beauty. The rhythm matched the divine impulse in the cosmos, the movement of creation, the outgoing of the divine wisdom. It matched the calls to praise which were addressed to all beings of the universe. The dance was at the centre of things.

The outstanding dance of the Lord's anointed fitted the significance of dance as belonging to the highest moments of fellowship with God. As the servant-son is the foremost minstrel, so too he is prince of the dance.

The dance of thanksgiving and testimony was another example of mission and message in dancing, for this manifestation of joy was a sign to others and an invitation to taste and see how gracious the Lord is.

While there was bodily expression of grief and lamentation, and so a kind of dance of death, it is rather the dance of life that is most obvious in the Psalms. In the presence of the Lord, when the whole community was filled with joy beyond words, it remained to dance.

Drama

The festal music and dance, in a sense, were part of an acted story. The moods they express were not just turned on as performers produce moods for an arbitrary medley of pieces, or as a modern congregation sing hymns loud or soft, bright or sad, at the request of organist or vicar. Rather, the ancient worshippers wept or rejoiced because they had come to a particular part of the festal story, a sacred drama in which they were totally immersed. All 'acted' in it, but without artifice, for it was a symbol of their very life, a distillation of the deepest human experiences. The story concerned origin and destiny, the fight against evil, the replenishment of life. And it was a sacrament. The reality which it depicted was present in it. God and his kingdom were present. The symbols of renewal were the means of renewal.

The overarching theme of the chief festival was the revelation of God. This was our 'drama of revelation'. Scenes that were well represented in the Psalms included the Lord's defeat of chaos, his triumphal procession to his throne, the proclamation of the gospel of his kingdom, his manifestation in glory, and his speeches of promise, warning, and destiny in the new era. The poetry, the music and the dance all served in the enactment, and no less did the architecture. The action moved from point to point on the 'stage' of the holy precinct, its outlying stations and sacred way. The properly prepared place, with all the symbolism of its construction, helped to mediate the truth of the actions in all their sacramental power; it is the holy place that is addressed with the song 'All my fresh springs are in you'.

The main drama was supported by other dramatic enactments and sacraments. One set forth atonement and another bestowed blessing on Jerusalem's defences. Most interesting

155

was the sequence which established and showed the vocation of the king, 'the Lord's anointed'. In dramatic scenes this made clear how the Lord crowned a Representative on earth to execute his will, and how he would give him victory if he walked humbly and trustingly with God. The vivid scenes showed him anointed by God and so made 'holy', intimate with God; then given a written oracle which authorized him to rule as a son on behalf of his father; but showed him also as confronted by evil foes. Another scene presented him in lonely need pleading for God to come to his help, in consideration of his vow of loyalty and integrity. There were possible interpretations of other colourful texts, where the king may bear witness to his salvation from depths of symbolic suffering.

With all this I compared the sequence of Psalms 22 and 23, finding a fresh possibility for interpreting their mysteries. On any view, they could bear the reader through an experience of dramatic and prophetic force. In these psalms was hidden the deepest truth that could be known to the artist and prophet, a drama of death and resurrection in which every reader can still take part, joining with the Representative in his pilgrimage through the dark chasm to the fields and springs of life.

The arts and the Psalms
Art may be understood as an imitation of reality, a creation after creation, whereby the artist catches gleams of beauty or truth and holds them for our sharing. His gift of seeing more than most men benefits us all, as he leads us through the margins of his perception.

The ancient arts we have traced in the Psalms appeared at last to be various aspects of the one art. Its central work was to bring mankind into communion with the beauty that is the heart of all reality, the Lord himself. In forms of poetry, music and dance, drama was enacted; to enhance the symbolic meaning a stage was provided by architecture. Wherever art lives today, that work is continued; beauty is held for us in a small symbol, which draws us towards the great source.

Have we not found also that in the Psalms the ancient arts

156

still live? Yes, the springs flow fresh. They flow from One who speaks poetry, who delights to build beautifully, who leads the music, dance and drama at the heart of the world's meaning.

The singers also and trumpeters shall he rehearse.
All my fresh springs shall be in thee.

NOTES

Chapters 1 and 2
The works of the main contributors to modern psalm-research are described and assessed in my chapter in *Tradition and Interpretation* (ed. G.W. Anderson, Oxford, 1979), and, with a different standpoint, by E. Gerstenberger's chapter in *Old Testament Form Criticism* (ed. J.H. Hayes, San Antonio, 1974). Of commentaries, I would suggest for a beginning those by J.W. Rogerson and J.W. McKay (Cambridge, 1977), A.L. Ash and C.M. Miller (Austin, Texas, 1980), and my own (London, 1967). Interesting still in many ways is the fine commentary of A.F. Kirkpatrick (Cambridge, 1902).

The fullest collection of translated texts for comparison with the Old Testament is edited by J.B. Pritchard, *Ancient Near Eastern Texts* (Princeton, 3rd ed. 1969). He also edits the large collection of illustrations, *The Ancient Near East in Pictures* (Princeton, 2nd ed. 1969).

Further reading on Hebrew poetry can be found in S. Mowinckel's *The Psalms in Israel's Worship* (Oxford, 1962), especially ch.XIX; G.B. Gray's *Forms of Hebrew Poetry* (London, 1915); D.N. Freedman's *Pottery, Poetry and Prophecy* (Winona, Indiana, 1980) especially pp. 23–50.

Chapter 3
Among the excellent books of Kathleen Kenyon, *Digging up Jerusalem* (London, 1974) is most helpful for this chapter. Many points of archaeology can be followed up also in the *Encyclopaedia of Archaeological Excavations in the Holy Land* (ed. M.Avi Yonah, Oxford, 1975f.) and J. Gray's *I and II Kings* (London, 3rd ed. 1980).

Chapter 4

Enjoyable basic reading for this subject is offered in two books by Curt Sachs: *The History of Musical Instruments* (New York, 1940) and *The Rise of Music in the Ancient World* (New York, 1943). I have treated the subject with more detail, illustrations and references in an essay in a forthcoming volume of the series *Oudtestamentische Studiën* (ed. A.S. van der Woude, Leiden).

The record of the reconstructed Hurrian hymn is available with an explanatory booklet: Kilmer, Brown and Crocker, *Sounds from Silence; Recent Discoveries in Ancient Near Eastern Music* (Bit Enki publications, P.O. Box 9068, Berkeley, California 94709, 1976). Suzanne Haïk Vantoura's work is presented with cassette and a large book: *La Musique de la Bible Révélée* (Dessain and Tolra, Paris, 2nd edn. 1978). She has also issued musical booklets and records under the same title; for information, contact Fondation Roi David, 9 rue d'Artois, 75008 Paris.

Chapter 5

An interesting beginning on 'dance' can be made with Curt Sachs' *World History of the Dance* (New York, 1937). For basic and contemporary themes there is a readable treatment by Ted Shawm, *Dance We Must* (New York, 1974). The essays edited by J.G. Davies, *Dance and Worship* (Birmingham 1975) are out of print. They begin with a treatment by myself of dance in the O.T. (a shortened form of this essay appeared in the *Expository Times* vol.86, 1975, pp.136–40), and J. Lipner treats Indian dance and refers to Caitanya.

Chapter 6

In *Tradition and Interpretation* (see note on ch.1 above) I have outlined the contributions of Mowinckel, Johnson, Kraus and others to the study of the dramatic aspects of Israel's festivals. The main classic in English is A.R. Johnson's *Sacral Kingship in Ancient Israel* (Cardiff, 2nd ed. 1967).

Chapter 7

The works here quoted are my *Vision in Worship, The Relation of Prophecy and Liturgy in the O.T.* (London: SPCK, 1981, p.106); W. Sorell, 'Israel and the Dance' in *The Hebrew Impact on Western Civilisation* (ed. D.D. Runes, New York: The Philosophical Library, 1951, p.505); and Sam Keen, *To a Dancing God* (New York: Harper and Row, 1970, pp.160, 97).

SUBJECT INDEX

Schopenhauer, 146
Solomon, 47
Sorell, W., 145

Temple (see also Jerusalem), 61f, 150–52
Types, see Classes

Ugarit, 88

Wisdom, 36–37, 103
Work, 25–26

Zion, see Jerusalem

SCRIPTURE INDEX

164